VITTORIO EMMANUEL PARETO

THE
URBAN PLANNING
PAPERS

A SIMPLE MODEL TO EVALUATE URBAN
CONDITIONS

SOUTH SUDAN URBAN DEVELOPMENT
STRATEGY

THE URBAN COMPONENT OF THE
ENERGY CRISIS

DESIGNING AN ADDRESSING SYSTEM

SBN-13: 978-1543031126

ISBN-10: 1543031129

PRINTED IN THE USA BY CREATESPACE

Cover: View of Santa Teresa, Rio de Janeiro, by Chensiyuan.

https://commons.wikimedia.org/w/index.php?curid=10378857

In memoriam

Dr. José Picorelli and Morena Metello Bica,

my grandparents.

Table of Contents

i

A Simple Model to Evaluate Urban Conditions

Originally published on Habitat International (UK), Vol 16 No. 4, pp 99-117, Pergamon Press (London) 1992.

SSRN paper #2187315 (2009, 2013)

Introduction

One of the main objectives of urban planning is to promote and assure a comprehensive development process. To accomplish this purpose, several tasks are necessary, such as evaluating existing conditions, analyzing trends, establishing development strategies, defining goals, specifying projects and programs and allocating resources. The underlying assumption is that these projects and programs, when implemented, will upgrade the present pattern of urban conditions to an improved and more balanced pattern.

In practice, most urban projects and programs have a strong sectorial connotation, that reflects the urban administration structure. If there is no comprehensive planning activity, each agency will propose its own development scheme based on its perspective of the urban reality and set its own priorities and goals. In parallel, the sectors that are more visible to the public tend to obtain a larger share of the available resources, while the less visible must compete for the remaining resources, if any. A lack of water will raise an immediate outcry and demand resources, while vaccinating children for some disease or the maintenance of the drainage system often gets forgotten. Such an emotional, "first stage" decision making often creates serious distortions that aggravate the quality of life and require extraordinary resources to fix what could have been done properly and timely. Indeed, such process will tend to aggravate distortions and inequalities throughout the urban landscape. Within this scenario, the planning task should be guiding the resource allocation process and defining projects and programs according to the conditions found in each part of the city, focusing on reducing inequalities in the availability of urban equipment and on the distribution of public utilities and services.

Yet to reduce inequalities it is necessary to compare the current performance levels of each sector vis-à-vis the expected levels each sector should attain to improve the accessibility pattern to urban equipment, infrastructure, and services. Most sectorial agencies in the urban administration have their own development programs, which highlight their priorities, goals, and strategies. Assessing the effective demand for these programs is often difficult since resource allocation decisions tend to be subjective due to the lack of adequate means of comparison. How does one evaluate the need for better accessibility in one neighborhood, *vis-à-vis* the demand for improving the water supply at another? How does one balance the public transportation expansion with the school upgrading program? A more careful assessment of these issues is necessary to improve the resource allocation process and, ultimately, to attain higher public satisfaction with the results.

To dimension the degree to which each sector should improve its performance, it is necessary to evaluate the relative performance levels of all sectors. This is a challenging task. How does one identify and quantify the intensity and location of these actions? How does one assign resources among the several pressing issues? How does one evaluate the efficiency of the projects and programs in terms of achieving the original objectives? This paper discusses a method which would help to answer some of those questions and search for a better balance among the activities of the sectorial agencies throughout the urban space. By facilitating the assessment of the sectorial performance and establishing sectorial goals, it would help estimating the investment requirements by sector and by zone.

Assessing sectorial conditions by urban location is normally done by assembling and analyzing urban data. This is often discouraging. The data available for analysis are generally collected by several different agencies for their own specific objectives, frequently being either too general or too specific for planning purposes. Furthermore, the data sources rarely adopt the same spatial subdivision, since their information needs are based on their own operational characteristics. Data analysis can be especially difficult in the context of rapidly growing cities in developing regions, where data are often scarce, issues easily confused and resources extremely limited. Yet it is exactly in this context and for these reasons that a quantitative method should be considered, assuring that the distribution of resources will be proposed in line with effective - and not the perceived - demand. Such an approach, when possible, would contribute to reducing existing distortions in the spatial distribution of urban equipment and services, by focusing investments in the sectors and places where the distortions are more acute.

The analytical tools available to planners are usually borrowed from related fields, ranging from economics and statistics to urban geography and business management. Baxter (1976), Chorley and Haggett (1976), and Krueckeberg and Silvers (1976) describe various concepts and analysis techniques commonly used in planning. Examples of simple yet efficient uses of quantitative techniques can be found in Oppenheim (1980), Spencer (1984) and Sweet (1985). The United Nations Center for Human Settlements (Habitat) developed an Urban Data Management System (1981), demonstrating that urban data management and modeling systems can be based on small data sets and still provide the level of insight required by planners.

Conventional office software and notebook computers can perform all the basic data analysis required for urban planning, including basic mapping. Yet the objective in strategic planning is not excessive number crunching, but having a broader view of the urban scenario, which is, in this planning phase, more important than processing large quantities of detailed information.

This paper will propose and discuss the embryo of a simple analysis system to select and display urban data, in a format that would facilitate appraising and quantifying the demand for sectorial improvements at each urban zone. This system would also facilitate the establishment of sectorial goals which, when attained, would fulfill a predefined urban development strategy. Finally, it would contribute to estimate the allocation of investment resources among the several sectors and thus help to quantify sectorial development programs.

The system proposed is based on using indicators to represent each urban sector. These indicators are derived from a small database, in which the information is aggregated by zone, thus providing the necessary spatial connotation. The indicators are then normalized, allowing direct comparison of the performance of each sector, in each zone. Displaying the normalized indicators in graphic format facilitates data analysis and the evaluation of urban conditions among sectors and zones. Once the relative needs of each area are appraised, the same model can be used interactively to visualize the effect of proposed strategies and the resulting demand for investment.

Urban Indicators

While there is no perfect way to represent the conditions of each urban sector, it is common practice to assume that the sector's situation can be appraised with reasonable accuracy by one or more indicators, which provide a close proxy of these conditions. It is normally accepted that the national development level can be represented by its income *per capita;* health conditions by infant mortality or life expectancy at birth; education by the literacy rate; and so on. While each indicator can only represent a limited aspect of their sector, altogether they are able to convey the overall level of performance of the sectors. This is because the sectoral indicators are usually closely interrelated. One rarely finds a developed health system that presents low life expectancy or high infant mortality. Or, likewise, an undeveloped region that has a high income per capita.

There is an immense amount of information that is collected regularly by various sectorial agencies. Yet not all data are suitable to be used as indicators. Indicators should be chosen to represent reasonably well the performance of each selected sector. There may be cases where a single indicator does not properly represent its sector. In such case, it would be more appropriate to create a compound indicator, aggregating the more relevant aspects of the sector. For comparative purpose, the resulting value will represent better the performance of the sector than any of the individual factors by itself.

As an example, the performance of the water supply system could be assessed by a combination of two indicators, such as the ratio of dwellings with piped water supply and the volume of water supplied per capita per day. There is no point in having a decent supply of water if restricted to only some of the dwellings. In this hypothetical case, a simple compound indicator could be generated by using the product of these two indicators. If in one zone 85% of the dwellings have piped water and the volume of water delivered is 60 liters *per capita* per day, the "new" water indicator would be 51. Likewise, if another zone has only 40% of dwellings with piped water, receiving 100 liters *per capita* per day, the value of its water indicator will be 40. In this example, the water supply system of the latter zone would be relatively worse than the former. If some factors are more important than others, a weighing system may also be introduced, so that the final value reflects reasonably well the apparent sectorial conditions throughout the city.

Dividing the city into zones is necessary to assess the urban conditions throughout the city. In principle. the zoning should refer to existing neighborhoods and be as homogeneous as possible. Data must be available for all the spatial subdivisions (zones) of the city, otherwise, their conditions cannot be compared. This may be the main obstacle to overcome in obtaining urban data. Most data collecting agencies define their geographical subdivisions according to their own operational characteristics and these areas often do not coincide with the subdivisions adopted by other agencies. Furthermore, some sectors do not aggregate their information by area, but by network. Despite these constraints, it is usually possible to conceive a zoning system for which sectorial data are available or can be assembled without much effort.

Many informative indicators can be assembled from the available data, representing well the urban context. For our purpose, the indicators used can be limited to the sectors that are controlled or directly influenced by the urban administration - such as land use, housing, infrastructure, local services, transportation, education, health and environmental quality. Although other indicators may be very interesting, if an aspect is beyond the local government's sphere of competence, it cannot be addressed by local projects or programs and therefore is redundant for this purpose. To identify and dimension urban projects, the indicators selected should represent issues that can be improved by the local government, through its own financial and regulatory means, and by other levels of competence, that could be induced to participate in the process.

In practice, the group of indicators and the spatial subdivision system adopted tend to be a compromise between the relevance of the issue and the availability and representativeness of data. In Karachi[1], where this method was originally conceived, the city was divided into 58 analysis zones which were reasonably homogeneous for planning purposes. The typology of land use and characteristics of each zone were further assessed by satellite and aerial

1   Karachi Development Plan UNCHS/KDA/PADCO/PEPAC (1989).

photographs, which were used as an aid to interpolate data from other agencies using different spatial subdivisions. The indicators selected for this project represented urban sectors such as economy (income per household and ratio of unemployment), housing (number of households per dwelling, ratio of formal and informal housing), water supply (ratio of dwellings with piped water and volume of water distributed *per capita*), sewer system (ratio of dwellings with sewers), power supply (ratio of dwellings with electricity), gas system (ratio of dwellings with gas), communications (ratio of lines per dwelling), transportation (time of travel), education (school attendance), health (distribution of health facilities), recreation (recreational area *per capita*), security (number of incidents *per capita*), and environment (water and air pollution, noise levels). Data were obtained from a variety of sources, including a few surveys promoted by the Karachi Development Authority.

To evaluate the performance of a selected zone for a chosen sector, the simplest way is to compare the value of the indicator of that zone with the preferred benchmark for that sector. If one zone receives an average of 60 liters of water *per capita* and another receives 100, these indicators immediately convey the information that the performance of the latter is better than the former. Yet this information does not show if the water supply is generous, meager, or barely adequate. To assess the sectorial performance, it is necessary to select a benchmark to which the value of the indicators can be compared. If the standard adopted for an adequate distribution is 50 liters *per capita* per day, then both zones would have adequate performances. However, if the recommended volume is 400 liters *per capita*, then both zones are very poorly serviced. Thus, the choice of a suitable benchmark is essential for the analysis.

Adopting an external parameter, such as an international standard or the national mean, poses a problem. Such standards are often unattainable or inappropriate by the prevalent economic or physical context. Local factors can strongly affect the performance of each sector, such as economic conditions, cultural patterns, technological level, the physical availability of the resource considered and its distribution conditions.

Specific conditions of the city, such as topography, distance to supply centers or population density can facilitate the performance of some sectors while restraining others. Furthermore, the demand tends to be more influenced by the performance levels of neighboring zones than by external standards. Emotionally, the benchmark is usually the next-door neighbor, not an abstract, arbitrary value considered to be "adequate", "sufficient" or "minimum".

For instance, if the highest supply level in the city is 100 liters *per capita* per day, the zone that has that level is the best serviced and thus has a lower claim for improvements than any other zone, even if the value of its indicator is substantially lower than a recommended standard. External standards are very useful as a general parameter but not as the preferred benchmark.

But then, which benchmark should be used? Possibly, the best benchmark for a sector would be the average of the whole town. In principle, the zones that are above average are better off, while the zones that are under average are worse off. Using the urban average[2] as a benchmark has the unique advantage of being a local value, resulting from the specific local factors such as geography, economics, and even culture.

To be sure, the indicator of each zone is the average obtained for that zone. We are now comparing the average of the zone

2   The average or mathematical mean is obtained by adding the values of all elements and dividing by the number of elements.

(indicator) to the average of the town, our chosen benchmark for the considered sector. If the supply of water is 80 liters per household in the zone and the urban average is 110 liters per household, the water supply indicator for that zone would be .73, becoming comparable to the indicator of any other zone, calculated in the same way. Thus, the relative performance for all zones for a chosen sector can be easily compared and mapped.

We still need to find a way to evaluate the performance among different sectors. How can one compare water supply with environmental pollution, literacy or quality of public transportation? To do that we must normalize the indicators. By normalization, we eliminate the unit of measurement by transforming the data into new scores, with the mean of zero and a standard deviation of one[3]. Recall that the standard deviation of a set of scores shows the dispersion of these scores around their mean. The mean (M), or average, is the sum of all values (Y) divided by the number of values (N):

$$M = \frac{\Sigma Y}{N}$$

The standard deviation for the score, represented by σ is the square root of the sum of the square of the differences between each score and the mean, divided by the number of scores minus one:

$$\sigma = \sqrt{\frac{\Sigma (Yn - M)^2}{N - 1}}$$

To normalize the set of scores using the standard deviation, we divide the difference between each score and the mean by the standard deviation. Thus, a set of N scores (indicators), each denoted

3   The normalized scores are called Z-scores.

as Yn, whose mean is equal to M and whose standard deviation is σ, is transformed to a Z-score as:

$$Zn = \frac{Yn - M}{\sigma}$$

That's all there is to it. It can be shown that a set of Z-scores has a mean of zero and a standard deviation of one. Therefore, Z-scores are a unit-free measure that can be used to compare measurements made with different units – i.e. allowing to compare oranges with bananas.

When the indicators are normalized (i.e. transformed to Z-scores) they will indicate precisely the relative performance of each sector at each zone, regardless if in one sector the original unit is a percentage, another is the number of water connections, or the time of travel.

Thus, by comparing the normalized values of the indicators, the sectorial 'needs' of each zone can be evaluated. Furthermore, by ranking and evaluating the relative performance of each sector and zone through different periods of time it is possible to monitor the process of development of each zone, and appraise the effect of specific policies, projects, and programs. This technique also allows the quantification of the goals that should be attained to achieve the desired distribution of performance levels, making it easier to establish goals, define projects and allocate resources.

The procedure required to normalize the zonal indicators is quite simple. As mentioned above, the normal value of the indicator is obtained by calculating the difference between the value of each zonal indicator and the mean for the sector, and dividing the result by the standard deviation of the sector[4].

The values of the normalized indicators can be presented in a table, with columns representing the sectorial indicators and rows the spatial units (zones). Each column will represent a sectorial profile - the various performance levels for that sector throughout the city. Likewise, each row will represent a zonal profile - all the sectorial performance levels in that zone. These profiles can be displayed in graphic format, making it easier to visualize the variation of urban conditions by zone and by sector.

Implementing an Urban Assessment System

Structure of the system

A simple urban assessment system can be built using a conventional spreadsheet. This option allows great flexibility and very convenient for data entry and updating, as well as the easy generation of graphics and tables for analysis. Since all the data and programs can be stored in the spreadsheet and be linked together, every time the data are revised all recalculations are done automatically and the results are updated.

The basic system is composed of three matrices that have a similar format. The first, the 'basic data' matrix, is used as the main database, storing all the sectorial data needed to build the indicators. All data input is made into this matrix. If we decide to use as a representative indicator the recreational area per capita, then the data matrix should hold the recreational area and the number of inhabitants of the zones. If a percentage, such as the literacy ratio,

---

4   This procedure assumes a normal distribution of the data, which should be expected for these types of data.

then we should have, in the data matrix, columns for the number of literate adults and the total number of adults for each zone.

The 'urban indicators' matrix, will hold the formulas to calculate the indicators and thus will display the complete set of indicators, based on the values of the database matrix. The third, the 'normalized indicator' matrix, will calculate and display the normalized values of the indicators to be compared.

The three matrices have the same basic format: the rows identify the zones and the columns identify the specific attributes. As such, all three will have the same number of rows - one for each zone. The number of columns of the basic database will be the same as the number of data items needed to calculate the indicators.

The indicator matrix has the same format, the columns displaying the sectoral indicators. It is convenient to add two auxiliary rows, to calculate the mean and the standard deviation of each indicator[5], which will be necessary to calculate the values of the normalized data matrix.

The normalized data matrix is like the indicator matrix, but holds the normalized value of each indicator for each zone.

Report generation is easily achieved by the spreadsheet application itself, though the data tables and graphs.

While for most indicators a positive and higher value indicates better conditions, for some a negative value represents a better performance. This would be the case for indicators such as time of travel, when a lower value indicates a more efficient transportation system. To facilitate analyzing the profiles, the normalized indicators in which lower values represent better

---

5   The formula used to calculate the standard deviation is: SD=@SQRT(@COUNT(list)/(@COUNT(list)–1)*@VAR (list)).

performances should be multiplied by minus one. This inversion will assign positive values to all sectors with better performances so that they will be displayed in the upper part of the charts.

Implementing the system

The first step in setting up this urban assessment system is to define the number of spatial units (zones), and select the indicators that will be used to assess the urban conditions in those zones. The sectorial indicators will determine the data items that will be required. Once the number of zones, the data items, and the indicators are defined, the spreadsheet matrices can be assembled, and data can be entered in the system. The values of the indicators, in both standard and normalized formats, are automatically computed and displayed.

A simplified example of the three matrices that compose the system is shown in the following pages, representing a hypothetical city divided into 12 planning zones.

Table 1 displays the basic database input matrix, containing all data necessary to run the system. Table 2 shows the indicator matrix, where the values of the indicators, the mean and the standard deviation are calculated for all sectors. Finally, Table 3 displays the normalized values of the indicators, which are used to draw the graphs for each indicator (sector profiles) and for each zone (zonal profiles).

In this example, the indicator for housing conditions is represented by the ratio of informal dwellings. This indicator is calculated by dividing the number of informal dwellings by the total number of dwellings (sum of formal and informal dwellings). The condition of the water supply system is represented by the ratio of dwellings with water connection, calculated by dividing the total number of dwellings with water connection by the total number of dwellings. The indicators for the other infrastructure systems, such as

15

sewers, electrically and telephone, are calculated in a similar way. The indicator for the transportation system is represented by the average time of travel divided by the distance to the center of employment. Education is represented by the ratio of primary school enrolment, obtained by dividing the number of pupils enrolled by the total school-age population. Finally, the sectors of health and recreation are assessed by the ratio of health facilities *per capita* and the recreational area *per capita*, respectively. To facilitate describing the system, no aggregated indicators were used and no attempt was made to use a weighing system to balance the relative importance of each. In practice, however, both alternatives should be considered.

Zone	Population	School Age Population	Area	Formal Dwellings	Informal Dwellings	Dwellings with Water	Dwellings w/ Sewer	Dwellings w/ Electr.	Dwellings w/ Tel	Travel Time to Centre	Distance to Centre	Primary Enrolment	Health Centres	Recreation Area
1	12,500	1,200	90	2,250	250	2,300	1,400	2,400	1,150	3.00	0.50	900	8.00	4.00
2	24,200	7,200	140	3,600	900	3,700	3,000	4,400	2,600	18.00	2.50	6,500	9.00	5.00
3	35,100	12,000	270	4,250	2,100	4,500	2,300	6,200	3,800	20.00	3.00	10,400	12.00	7.00
4	8,500	2,300	45	1,050	250	1,100	800	1,250	1,000	10.00	1.00	1,800	4.00	1.00
5	18,300	5,400	120	3,150	340	3,200	2,700	3,400	2,400	35.00	4.20	4,800	9.00	1.00
6	45,300	10,200	270	8,000	1,800	8,200	6,500	9,600	6,400	45.00	5.70	8,200	12.00	5.00
7	24,900	7,200	140	2,400	2,100	2,500	1,200	4,300	1,200	17.00	2.30	6,500	13.00	12.00
8	37,700	9,800	180	5,250	1,200	5,350	4,500	6,300	2,300	10.00	1.40	7,500	15.00	12.00
9	23,500	6,800	210	3,700	100	3,750	3,600	3,600	1,200	10.00	1.40	5,200	12.00	10.00
10	19,400	5,800	180	3,400	800	3,900	3,850	3,900	1,200	34.00	3.70	4,800	10.00	13.00
11	8,700	2,800	48	1,400	600	1,650	1,500	1,900	500	8.00	0.90	2,500	5.00	3.00
12	21,800	7,400	234	3,600	500	3,800	3,650	3,800	900	39.00	5.60	6,500	8.00	9.00
Total	279,900	78,100	1,927	42,050	10,940	43,950	35,000	51,050	24,650	20.75	2.68	65,600	117.00	82.00

Figure 1 - Data base matrix

17

Zone	Proportion Informal Dwelling (%)	Proportion Dwelling w/ water (%)	Proportion Dwelling w/ sewer (%)	Proportion Dwelling w/ Electr. (%)	Proportion Dwelling w/ phone (%)	Travel Time / Km	Proportion Prim. School Attendance (%)	Health Centre /10,000	Recreation Area /10,000
1	10.00	92.00	56.00	96.00	46.00	6.00	75.00	6.40	3.20
2	20.00	82.22	66.67	97.78	57.78	7.20	90.28	3.72	2.07
3	33.07	70.87	36.22	97.64	59.84	6.67	86.67	3.42	1.99
4	19.23	84.62	61.54	96.15	76.92	10.00	78.26	4.71	1.18
5	9.74	91.69	77.36	97.42	68.77	8.33	88.89	4.92	0.55
6	18.37	83.67	66.33	97.96	65.31	7.89	80.39	2.65	1.10
7	46.67	55.56	26.67	95.56	26.67	7.39	90.28	5.22	4.82
8	18.60	82.95	69.77	97.67	35.66	7.14	76.53	3.98	3.18
9	2.63	98.68	94.74	94.74	31.58	7.14	76.47	5.11	4.26
10	19.05	92.86	91.67	92.86	28.57	9.19	82.76	5.15	6.70
11	30.00	82.50	75.00	95.00	25.00	8.89	89.29	5.75	3.45
12	12.20	92.68	89.02	92.68	21.95	6.96	87.84	3.67	4.13
Average	20.65	82.94	66.05	96.34	46.52	7.73	83.99	4.18	2.93
STD	11.89	11.60	20.81	1.86	19.50	1.16	5.96	1.08	1.78

Figure 2 - Indicator matrix

Zone	Inf. Dwel.	Water	Sewer	Electricity	Telephone	Transport	Education	Health	Recreation	Sum
1	0.8951	0.7809	-0.4830	-0.1819	-0.0266	1.4934	-1.5085	2.0559	0.1517	3.1771
2	0.0543	-0.0619	0.0296	0.7723	0.5773	0.4593	1.0537	-0.4270	-0.4846	1.9730
3	-1.0448	-1.0407	-1.4335	0.6972	0.6832	0.9189	0.4481	-0.7050	-0.5249	-2.0015
4	0.1189	0.1444	-0.2168	-0.0993	1.5590	-1.9538	-0.9616	0.4870	-0.9839	-1.9062
5	0.9168	0.7542	0.5437	0.5809	1.1408	-0.5174	0.8208	0.6834	-1.3375	3.5857
6	0.1915	0.0632	0.0133	0.8697	0.9683	-0.1395	-0.6042	-1.4179	-1.0247	-1.0853
7	-2.1880	-2.3603	-1.8926	-0.4205	-1.0179	0.2944	1.0537	0.9639	1.0605	-4.5066
8	0.1716	0.0005	0.1786	0.7169	-0.5568	0.5085	-1.2518	-0.1864	0.1422	-0.2767
9	1.5147	1.3570	1.3785	-0.8600	-0.7660	0.5085	-1.2619	0.8579	0.7440	3.4727
10	0.1343	0.8547	1.2310	-1.8689	-0.9202	-1.2550	-0.2073	0.9026	2.1166	0.9878
11	-0.7866	-0.0379	0.4301	-0.7187	-1.1033	-0.9962	0.8873	1.4513	0.2911	-0.5830
12	0.7105	0.8397	1.1040	-1.9625	-1.2596	0.6624	0.6445	-0.4726	0.6728	0.9393

Figure 3 - Normalized indicators matrix

Analyzing urban conditions

Although relative urban conditions can be directly assessed by analyzing the values of the normalized indicators, it is easier and faster to view the sectorial and zonal profiles in graphic format. In this example, bar charts for all sectorial and zonal profiles were generated through the spreadsheet application. The vertical bars display the normalized values of indicators representing the sector or zone. These values can be positive or negative, corresponding to performance levels higher or lower than the urban mean. As the urban mean of normalized indicators is always zero, values near the center line indicate average performance conditions, while high positive or negative values indicate distribution distortions - unusually high or low performance levels.

The sector profiles display the performance levels of a chosen sector throughout the urban space. While bar charts allow identifying the sectors with low-performance conditions, it Is often more illustrative to display the relative conditions in the more traditional map format. This can be done by adopting a ranking system and generating theme maps for each sector. A five-level ranking system is often enough, displaying very good, good, average, bad and very bad performance levels. The map format allows one to visualize where the urban conditions demand prompt action. The following figure shows the water supply sector profile in a map format, using the data from the example.

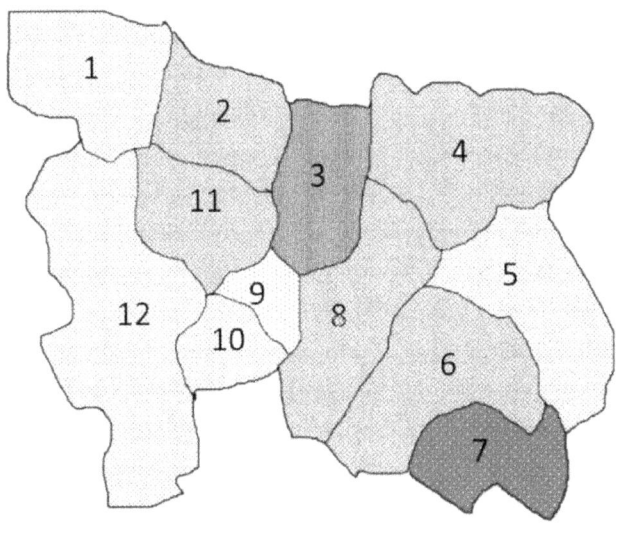

Legend:

Zone 9	very good
Zones 1, 5, 10, 12	good
Zones 2, 4, 6, 8, 11	average
Zone 3	bad
Zone 7	very bad

Figure 4- Water supply sector (map format)

Figures 5 and 6 illustrate the profiles of zones 7 and 2 from the example:

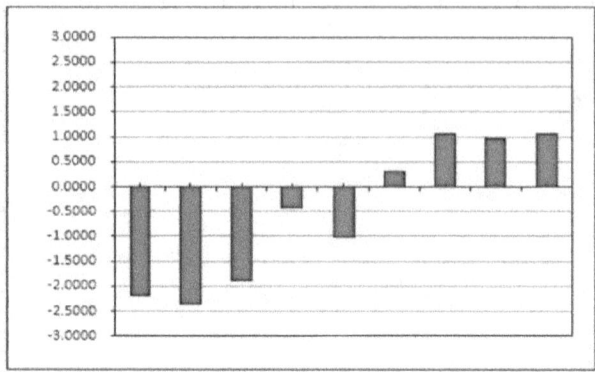

Figure 5 - Profile zone 7

Zone 7 presents low-performance levels in the housing and infrastructure sectors (indicators 1, 2, 3), although the performance in the other sectors is acceptable or better than average. Thus, the situation of housing and infrastructure deserves further analysis to identify the causes of the situation and the actions that would be suitable to improve these conditions.

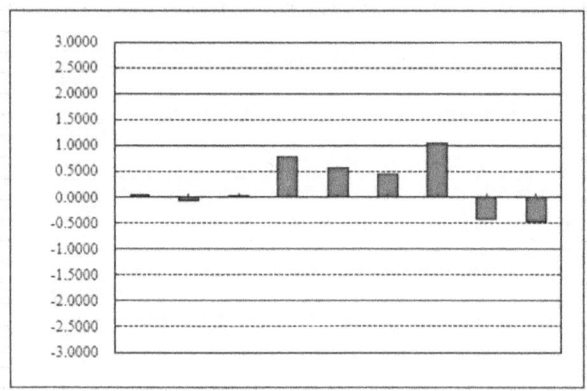

Figure 6 - Profile zone 2

Zone 2, on the contrary, does not seem to have any significant issue. All indicators are reasonably near or above the urban mean.

The following Figures 7 and 8 illustrate two sectorial profiles, displaying the conditions of housing and water supply (represented by the distribution of informal dwellings and the number of water connections). The housing profile highlights that the housing issue is more acute in zone 7, followed by zones 3 and 11. In the same way, the water supply system is extremely deficient in zones 7 and poor in zone 3. In a similar way, all zones and sectors should be analyzed, identifying the critical issues and their spatial location.

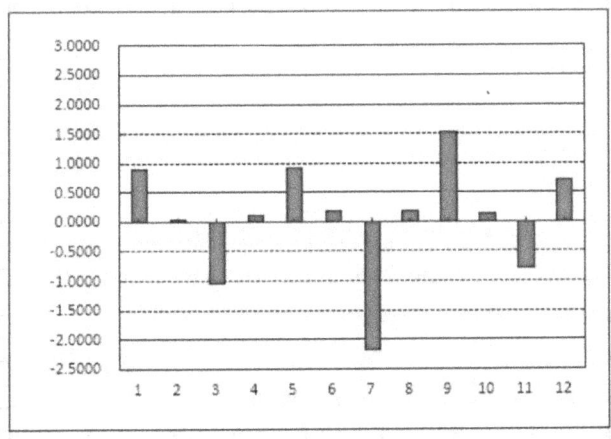

Figure 7 - Housing profile

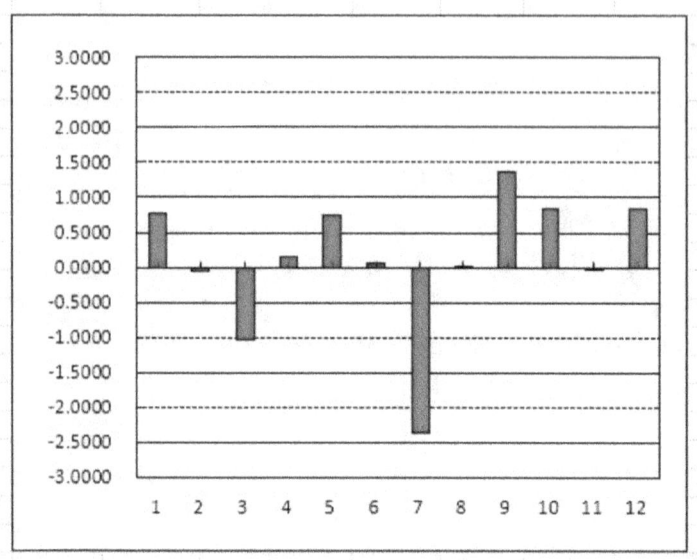

Figure 8 - Water supply profile

One of the main advantages of using zonal profiles to analyze urban conditions is the possibility of displaying the spatial distribution of the relative performance of each sector in a compact format. This characteristic allows the rapid visualization of critical issues and their location. However, using urban indicators as proxies for the various urban sectors cannot be expected to represent with great precision any issue. Furthermore, since the zonal values are the average for each zone, a heterogeneous distribution within that zone will not be noticed. As such, before dimensioning sectorial actions or development programs, the target areas and issues in question should be examined in detail, considering the specific aspects and circumstances prevailing in each area.

Development strategies

After identifying the main issues and their locations, it is necessary to define a policy to deal with these issues. It would be unrealistic to suppose that the prevailing urban conditions could be raised much beyond the average levels found in similar cities, or much above the urban national average. If such a policy is adopted, not only will it require massive investments - probably beyond the local financing capacity - but it will also attract migration from other centers which will tend to revert the urban conditions to the previous levels.

More pragmatic alternatives might be to consider establishing policies which aim to raise the zonal conditions below average to the urban mean, or to another pre-established level. This process by itself will raise the average conditions of the city. Another policy could establish that all zones should be improved, by a fixed percentage or by a variable rate aiming to reduce zonal inequalities. The latter policy could be implemented by directing self-financing schemes to the 'best' zones and concentrating public investments on improving the 'worst' areas. These examples are only some of the options for establishing urban development policies.

Development policies may focus on alleviating current issues, such as environmental quality, social development, public transportation or infrastructure, or be defined according to prevalent political trends.

Variations in the urban conditions are assessed by changes in the values of the indicators. When new data are entered in the input matrix the performance indicators are automatically calculated. Therefore, the system can be used interactively, by modifying the data at the input matrix until the desired pattern of performance levels is obtained. These selected changes could then become the initial development objectives.

Defining development goals

An urban development program obviously should not focus on simply improving the aspects used in the indicators. The actions proposed must be comprehensive and reflect local conditions, opportunities and constraints that cannot be shown only through the indicators. Furthermore, a program to enhance the water system at one place may also be used to improve neighboring areas at a marginal cost. On the other hand, there are thresholds of supply that must be observed. Power plants, telephone exchanges, water supply lines, roads, bridges, schools, parks, etc. all have standard production capacities or more economical dimensions that must be considered when defining development goals. Therefore, the goals resulting from local conditions need to consider the physical, economical and operational opportunities and constraints.

It is important to stress that improving a sector, as for instance the electrical supply system, does not mean merely increasing the number of electrical connections, but comprehensively upgrading the whole system: from power generation and transmission to energy conversion and local distribution, as required to satisfy the established goals. Since the comprehensive upgrading of each system has inherent industrial and operational thresholds, this factor should have a major influence in the establishment of the sectorial goals, aiming to achieve more cost-effective programs.

Conclusions

The system discussed is reasonably simple to implement, requires relatively few data and can provide a basic guideline to dimension development projects. As such, it can be a valuable tool to discuss planning alternatives. The major obstacle to overcome is to assure that each zone is reasonably homogeneous so that the zonal indicators can reflect reasonably well the existing conditions.

While the example presented was made simple for demonstration purposes, only the availability of data limits prevents expanding the system to more complex levels. One such option could be incorporating cost functions, reflecting cost variations, operational thresholds, and other factors. If the model is extended, it is preferable to build independent modules so that the results can be appraised separately. These modules could eventually be linked together to present consolidated results. This procedure would allow more control over the system, avoiding distortion in the results from possible data errors or programming limitations.

Sources and References

Baxter, R.: Computer and Statistical Techniques for Planners. Methuen, London, 1976.

Chorley, R. and Haggett, P. (Editors): *Socio-Economic Models in Geography*. Methuen, London, 1976.

Gordon, A. D.: Classification: Methods for the Exploratory Analysis of Multivariate Data. Chapman & Hall, London, 1987.

Hartigan, J.: *Clustering Algorithms*. Wiley, New York, 1975.

Jain, A. and Dubes, R.: *Algorithms for Clustering Data*. Prentice Hall, Englewood Cliffs, New Jersey, 1988.

Kaufman, L.: *Finding Groups in Data*. Wiley, New York, 1990.

Kelley, A.: *Modelling Urbanization and Economic Growth*. IIASA, Laxenburg, Austria, 1980.

Kovach, W.: *Multivariate Statistical Package*. Bloomington, Indiana, 1985.

Krueckeberg, D. and Silvers, A.: *Urban Planning Analysis: Methods and Models*. John Wiley, New York, 1976.

Mohan, R.: Urban Economic and Planning Models - Assessing the Potential for Cities in the Development Countries. John Hopkins

University Press, Baltimore, 1979.

Oppenheim, N.: *Applied Models in Urban and Regional Analysis*. Prentice Hall, Englewood Cliffs, New Jersey, 1980.

Pareto, V. E. et al.: *Karachi Development Plan,* KDA/UNCHS/PADCO, Karachi, 1989.

Spencer, R.: *Cluster Analysis*, BYTE, September 1984.

Sweet, H.: *The Use of Clustering Techniques on an Apple Computer*, The American Biology Teacher, January 1985.

South Sudan Urban Development Strategy

Published on Alliance Journal Business Research, Bangalore, July 2009; SSRN paper #1285243.

Introduction

This working paper was based on an urban planning study developed in 2006 to support a rapid deployment infrastructure development program being prepared by Gibb Africa, KweziV3, and PADCO-AECOM for the Government of South Sudan (GOSS).

Developing an urban structure is critical to the economic development of Southern Sudan. Yet currently the basic building blocks needed for development – institutional structure, financial system, health and education infrastructure, human resources, active private sector and economic activities, and an operating inter-urban transportation system – are either missing or still at an embryonic stage. While some of these shortcomings can be dealt with in short-term, others will require a longer period to attain a satisfactory level, especially those involving human resources and social development.

The lack of basic statistics and the turbulent pre-Comprehensive Peace Agreement (CPA) period makes it difficult to establish trends and estimate future urban growth. Currently, it is assumed that only 10% of the population is urbanized. Even if the overall population doubles with the return of internally displaced persons (IDP) and returning refugees (RR), and if a significant part settles in the state capitals, the population should continue to be overwhelmingly rural within the foreseeable future. Rural development is a national priority, yet it needs an operational urban system to provide essential supporting services.

The estimated population growth in the 10 state capitals is expected to double in the next five years. Catering to this extraordinary influx will require substantial investment in basic infrastructure – not only to upgrade the current towns but to provide developed land equivalent to double the existing built up area. After this growth surge the cities probably continue to grow, yet probably at a substantially lower rate. The most critical period is the immediate period.

The urgent priority is upgrading the cities to a basic, yet fully operational level to perform their economic support functions; and providing basic infrastructure services to the current population and the migrants (IDPs and RRs) expected in short term.

Given the logistics required to meet these priorities, the development effort should be divided into three distinct, consecutive phases:

- A first phase, already under way, comprising emergency works and road recovery programs, which together should jump-start the development process;
- The second phase should be a short-term urban consolidation phase, enabling all basic 'state capital' functions and improving urban standards;
- The third would be a long-term urban expansion phase, during which most urban infrastructure expansion and socio-economic development would take place and improved standards would be progressively extended to the whole city.

This development strategy focuses on resolving the logistic and implementation issues progressively, each phase based on the work done in the previous phase. Even so, upgrading the cities and doubling their size in such a short period will put an enormous demand on the available resources.

Responding to this demand on a financially sustainable basis, the urban development strategy should concentrate the development effort during the short-term consolidation phase on building a "city core", to attain a 'state capital' operational level as soon as possible. The standards to be applied in the city core and the residential neighboring areas must be contingent on realistic affordability levels so assure sustainability. Thus, the initial residential

32

neighborhood standards should be limited to improving the access to "safe water", public sanitation and electricity. Even so, this will be a significant and highly visible improvement on the current conditions.

The planning of the short-term consolidation phase should include project briefs on priority land development and infrastructure works. This short-term plan should contain institutional strengthening guidelines, including initiatives to build up the capacity of the local governments for implementation related tasks.

The long-term urban expansion plan should provide guidelines for the progressive expansion of higher infrastructure service standards to the entire urban center, providing all the urban population with improved services and living conditions. The expansion phase assumes that higher affordability levels are attained so that sustainability will continue to be ensured.

Ideally, the proposed long-term planning guidelines should be reviewed at the end of the short-term plan, when a better information base on demographic socio-economic trends is available and further economic development opportunities are identified.

All the urban development plans should include three main components:

- A physical development component, focusing on land use, housing, land allocation, building, water supply, sanitation, waste management, electrical supply and road improvements;

- An institutional development program, providing guidelines for institutional building and strengthening; and

- A capital investment and implementation schedule, outlining the required financial inputs to the implementation effort.

Finally, the urban development strategy proposes general planning recommendations on housing and land use, the city core, urban and socio–economic services, traffic, and environment.

Background

The purpose of this paper is to present the development of a sustainable, affordable and realistic urban development strategy that can respond to the immediate needs of GOSS[1], to minimize the lack of an urban structure capable of supporting a comprehensive economic development effort, to provide shelter for IDPs[2], RRs[3], and rural migrants, and to improve the living condition of the current residents. The initial work focuses on the future state capitals. Some of them already are sizable towns, although most without infrastructure or services. Others are smaller settlements, and a few will have to be built from scratch.

Southern Sudan is currently an autonomous, self-governing region of the Republic of Sudan and is the result of a Comprehensive Peace Agreement (CPA) that ended 22 years of bitter civil war (1983-2005). Since the independence of Sudan fifty years ago (1956), Southern Sudan only had 10 years of unstable peace. Old buildings and structures left by the British were bombed and destroyed during the two long civil wars, and the continuous warfare prevented any urban development and infrastructure upgrading.

The population of Southern Sudan is almost entirely rural or semi-nomadic, herding cattle and living at subsistence level. Yet the economy of Southern Sudan is based on oil revenues, which under the CPA are shared with the Republic of Sudan. These revenues are to be used to finance the development of the new nation – it is

1   Government of South Sudan.
2   Internal Displaced Persons.
3   Returning Refugees.

assumed that the referendum of 2011 will favor the secession of Southern Sudan from the north, as widely expected.

The task of rebuilding the urban structure is made more difficult by the stage of development of the existing centers. It's not simply a question of providing infrastructure, identifying areas for development, or providing shelter to the IDPs. It is a matter of providing urban support to the social and the economic development of the country, which will have to focus in these ten urban centers. Of these, Juba, Wau, and Malakal have a reasonably large population, Juba rapidly being converted into the future national capital. Most of the other state capitals are rather small settlements (Rumbek, Bentiu-Rubkona, Aweil and Yambio), and the remaining are not much more than rural villages (Bor, Torrit, and Kapoeta)[4].

If the cities do not develop their own economic functions and their capacity to provide services, the economic development of Southern Sudan will be seriously compromised, and with it the hopes of providing a better future to its population. Urban development is thus an imperative to the national development of Southern Sudan.

Although there may be enough financial resources, the task of developing these cities is made difficult because the basic resources that are needed to trigger the development process are still not in place or exist only in an embryonic stage:

- the institutional context is weak and in some cases inexistent;
- the financial system is largely inexistent;
- the social infrastructure (education and health) is basically inexistent;

4   This study was done before independence, when the state capitals had not yet been formally designated.

- the current human resources are limited and skilled IDPs that might return may not want to settle in the current under-developed towns;

- there are no significant industrial or commercial activities, neither an active private sector.

- there is no significant rural economic base. Except for oil extraction, in which the role of Southern Sudan is still very limited, there are no other significant economic activities; and

- neither the urban infrastructure nor the transportation network can currently support any significant economic development process.

Some of these shortcomings can be dealt with in short or medium term, given sufficient resources. Yet building human resources and adjusting living patterns from a rural subsistence level to a more modern urban context is a long process that may take decades to achieve.

There are also no reliable statistics to estimate socioeconomic and demographic trends. Much of the development process has to rely on 'educated guesses' on how the population will grow, on the rate of returning IDPs, on future employment opportunities, on the effects of better sanitation, water supply and electricity on the population growth and urban expansion, and so on. Thus, an urban investment planning approach must be based on a step by step process, each serving as support to the next. Such approach will minimize mistakes and allow making changes in the investment program in response to the effects obtained.

Yet the challenge of developing Southern Sudan's urban system, starting with the state capitals and progressively including the other regional urban centers, presents a unique opportunity to build up the urban backbone that is required for the social and economic development of the nation.

The development challenges.

Currently, Southern Sudan has an estimated population of around 8-10 million people – no reliable figure is available – and the 10 state capitals have, altogether, not over a million inhabitants, about 10% of the assumed total population. This indicates that Southern Sudan is an overwhelmingly rural country and, regardless of a probable short-term urbanization trend, should keep that characteristic in the foreseeable future.

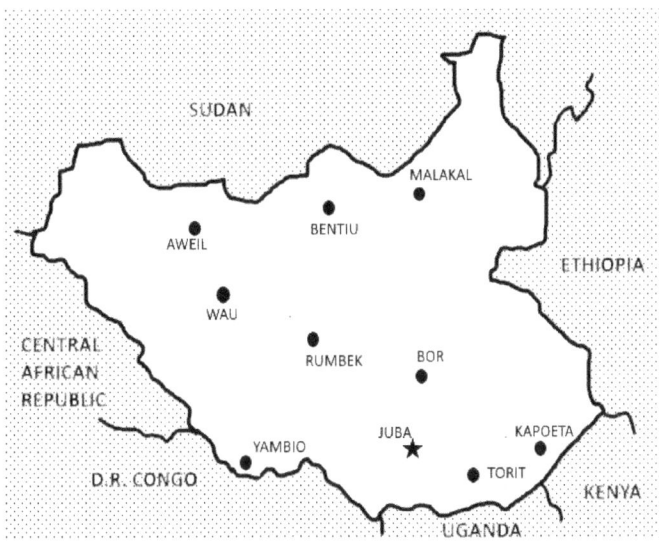

Figure 9 - South Sudan state capitals.

Nevertheless, it is essential to establish a basic urban network to support the social and economic development of the rural population – functions that can only be performed from an urban base. Urban areas are the focus of economic activities and provide a higher per capita contribution to the national production, due to the higher levels of productivity and performance. Furthermore, they also provide a more diversified employment base and income

37

earning opportunities than rural areas, as well as higher educational and health service levels, which support both urban and rural populations. The urban environment also provides greater and more diversified opportunities for female education, employment, and income, reducing the gender inequities related to the Sudanese Islamic culture. The development of the urban system also decentralizes the development processes, improving the accessibility of the population – urban and rural – to better living conditions, even if still quite basic at first.

Additionally, agricultural development relies on services that are can only be available in well-functioning urban service centers. Thus, the development of a basic urban network is critical to increase rural productivity and to progressively improve the living conditions of the inhabitants of smaller towns and rural villages, reducing the inequities between urban and rural areas.

Estimating the probable size of the state capitals – the basic nodes of the future urban network - is anything but precise or reliable - the current size is unknown and changes according to the season, as a considerable part of the population is made of semi-nomadic herders. Natural growth must be an educated guess, although it is expected to increase when sanitation conditions improve. The number of returning IDPs and RRs varies widely according to the agency making the assessment and it is quite uncertain where those returning will settle.

Urban Centre	2006	2011	2016	2021	% growth
Aweil	70	114	132	149	2.1
Yambio	65	108	128	147	2.3
Rumbek	85	153	182	210	2.5
Wau	220	409	490	591	2.6
Kapoeta	7	13	15	17	2.4
Torit	21	36	43	49	2.3
Bentiu/Rubkona	75	168	191	212	2.8
Juba	200	490	575	657	3.3
Malakai	140	359	421	480	3.4
Bor	12	57	73	91	7.6
TOTAL	895	1907	2250	2583	2.9
Average Growth(%)		2.1	2.5	2.9	
Additional Population		1012	343	333	

Figure 10 - Population Estimates 2006-2021 (1,000's)

A note should be made on how the numbers were generated. The current urban population was calculated based on the count of existing houses and huts and the average number of people living in each unit. The natural growth trend was estimated based on other African regions with similar characteristics, considering the probable influence of safe water and sanitation in infant survival rate (Lucius 2006).

The number of IDPs and RRs was based on the currently available UN estimates and the medium rate of returning families. It is generally assumed that the displaced population will return in force to Southern Sudan and this could bring the national population to over 15 million inhabitants. It is expected that a high proportion of the already urbanized population will settle in the more urbanized centers, such as Juba and the larger towns. It was also considered the added attraction of places with better accessibility and the influence of the ethnic profile of the IDPs and RRs on choosing the region they would prefer to resettle.

The development of an urban system itself should probably exert a strong influence on the demographic distribution. Natural growth in urban areas is expected to increase due to improved sanitation and health conditions, and migration from rural areas should increase, to benefit from urban services and take advantage of urban employment opportunities.

The expected rapid growth should increase dramatically the demand for urban land, infrastructure, and services. On the other hand, urban-based economic development should boost employment and income levels, and higher affordability will result in more people having access to better services and higher infrastructure standards.

Current Conditions

Southern Sudan is economically under-developed. There is little industrial activity and, besides oil extraction, it only shows a subsistence farming economy. The economic base of the towns is extremely weak and relies on the salaries of Southern Sudanese government's employees and of the Government of Sudan's military personnel. There are few businesses, banks are limited to the larger towns and local markets are small and poorly supplied.

The interurban transportation system that is currently being recovered does not offer all-weather conditions, constraining the supply of essential goods and the export of agricultural produce, which are limited to the few existing towns and their immediate surroundings.

This urban settlement context suggests a kind of self-sufficient 'city-state' scenario, where an administrative, commercial and residential core is supported by a peripheral agricultural area, with limited external inputs or outputs. Due to such limitations, there is little production to export to external markets or any significant employment besides government jobs.

The urban infrastructure situation is bleak – there is no access to safe water, no sanitation, no waste collection, no electricity and no means of communication. There are insufficient primary schools, no vocational schools, few and ill-equipped health facilities, no recreational areas.

Fortunately, there is plenty of available land for urban development and the urban road networks, having negligible traffic, are in reasonable conditions except where damaged by poor drainage. There are few sources of building materials available (timber, clay and sand) and all manufactured building products need to be imported from abroad.

The conventional benchmark for the provision of services – conditions of affordability and sustainability – cannot be directly applied in the towns of Southern Sudan, except within the government context itself: the government "consumer" paying for the services provided by the government "supplier".

The lack of economic activity and employment does not stimulate the establishment of modern banks or credit institutions. Housing is based on the provision of land by the local authorities and self-built 'tukuls'[5], while the lack of demand constrains business activities to a minimum. Construction businesses are scarce or inexistent and the provision of general services does not go much beyond simple repair shops at the markets.

---

5   A round hut, about 5-8 meters wide, without openings except for the entrance. The roof has a conic shape and is made of straw, while the circular wall has low height and is made of mud. A large roof overhand protects the wall from rain and sunshine and a small opening at the top allows hot air to flow out, reducing the internal heat.

While there are some infrastructure and services in the larger towns and even in some of the smaller centers, urban development is still embryonic. This general overview shows that the city building effort must be done from scratch, side by side with the on-going nation building effort.

Finally, it should be stressed that as the urban development challenge will require a large number of skilled and unskilled workers, this opportunity should not be lost by the Sudanese labor force. Nonetheless, local workers must still be trained to meet the manpower demand of the reconstruction process.

Development Strategy

There is much to be done in a short time and there should be attention on using efficiently the existing financial resources - which are not as inexhaustible as they tend to be considered.

The lack of reliable information makes long-term forecasts unreliable – it is not possible to establish any reasonable assessment of population or economic growth trends. Furthermore, the level of development is so low that it is impossible to predict how the economic system will perform.

Thus, a progressive development approach is advisable – initially, the essential issues should be dealt with, while the development strategy itself should be revised periodically throughout the implementation period to adjust to changing local conditions, development progress and new demands.

The first step has already been taken by GOSS, by initiating emergency works projects. Nothing can be done without a minimum infrastructure support and this is the main objective of that project, currently under design. Yet the emergency works project deals only with bare minimum basic infrastructure and repair works that are needed to provide an initial operational base. These works are indispensable and urgent, yet are insufficient to make the towns operate as state capitals or as economic centers.

To perform as the state capital, there are critical pre-requisites, such as human resources, housing, infrastructure, institutional structure, government facilities, communications, financial institutions, and supply markets. To develop these prerequisites, the towns must have a bare-minimum yet indispensable base: infrastructure, inter-urban transportation, building materials, electricity and basic communications. And, to support the operation of this base, the rural productivity must improve dramatically.

This scenario leads to a natural split of the planning development effort into three distinct phases:

- initial 'jump-start' phase (the current 'emergency works' project), to provide essential basic services;
- consolidation phase (a short-term development project, to enable all the minimum 'state-capital' functions; and
- expansion phase (a long-term urban development strategy), when most of the urban expansion and social-economic development would take place.

The current planning effort outlines the short-term development project and the long-term development strategy. The short-term development plan aims to:

- enable the towns to function as state capitals, i.e. become effective administrative and political centers;
- provide essential services to their populations; and
- provide the basic essential requirements to start the economic development process.

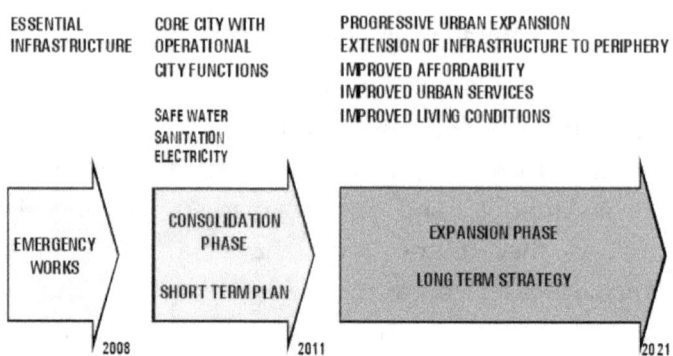

ESSENTIAL INFRASTRUCTURE | CORE CITY WITH OPERATIONAL CITY FUNCTIONS | PROGRESSIVE URBAN EXPANSION EXTENSION OF INFRASTRUCTURE TO PERIPHERY IMPROVED AFFORDABILITY IMPROVED URBAN SERVICES

SAFE WATER SANITATION ELECTRICITY | IMPROVED LIVING CONDITIONS

EMERGENCY WORKS

CONSOLIDATION PHASE

SHORT TERM PLAN

EXPANSION PHASE

LONG TERM STRATEGY

2008 · 2011 · 2021

The first phase is a comprehensive complement to the emergency works program – not only by expanding its scope in terms of enhancing the urban infrastructure and building government facilities, but also to build up the non-visible yet essential foundation for development: institutional building and strengthening, capacity building, and establishing the education and health infrastructure to meet the current demand.

In most cases, it will not be possible – due to resource and logistic constraints - to upgrade any entire town in one single effort. At present, due to such constraints, it is more realistic to focus on developing a 'city core' – a limited central area with improved conditions. The remaining informal urban area should bear lower standards, based on the capability to meet maintenance costs (essential for sustainability). Yet improving access to safe water and electricity in the whole urban area is as important as developing its urban core.

The 'city core' concept intends to assure the operation of essential government functions at state capital level – this would include the operation of government functions and services, the operation of the central social facilities (education and health units);

44

and the availability of land and provision of infrastructure support to the private sector.

The standards set for the city core must be sufficient to allow these objectives to be attained. It is expected that the existing economy, albeit weak, will be able to afford maintenance and operation costs.

The same level of standards can be extended to the adjoining areas based on affordability, such as the development of some housing areas. Yet the provision of services and infrastructure for the peripheral urban area should be contingent on the availability of resources to make the capital investment and the ability to sustain the services – both currently still unknown.

During the first development phase, preference should be given in consolidating the existing urban space – occupying empty areas and densifying the residential neighborhoods in line with the accepted affordable standards. The implementation of this policy will contribute to reducing the costs of providing infrastructure and services, thus increasing affordability levels and allowing the higher standards to be expanded from the city core to the whole urban area.

This recommendation should not interrupt the supply of urban land for development – new housing areas will be needed to cope with the expected increase in population during the period, especially considering the returning IDPs. In general, the population growth estimates suggest that the urban population of the 10 cities should more than double from 2006 to 2021, roughly requiring the urban area to expand at almost the same proportion.

It is expected that the first phase, which would take about 3-4 years to be implemented, could be started in 2007-2008 and expected to be completed by 2016[6]. Being conceived as an integrated short-term plan - although consistent with the longer development vision for each city – the short-term plan will describe with sufficient detail (as project briefs) the priority projects and activities to be undertaken, especially regarding the spatial and infrastructure development (physical and infrastructure plans), the social infrastructure, and the basic institutional backbone.

The long-term plan will cover the following 10-year period (2011-2020) providing comprehensive guidelines and recommendations for future urban development. It should consider the expected urban growth rate and higher income levels. It will provide guidelines to progressively upgrade the urban conditions, and cater for further development and urban expansion needs.

The long-term plan, however, should be re-evaluated at the end of the first phase, to correct eventual distortions and focus on possible unforeseen development issues and emerging opportunities.

By 2011 there will be a better information base from the planned census and it may be possible to re-evaluate the effective rate of return of IDPs, identify blossoming business enterprises, the growth in demand, and the attainment of higher affordability levels.

These factors will allow improving the basic 'city core' strategy proposed for the first 4-year phase and extending the city core standards to the whole urban area.

6   According to the CPA a referendum would be held in 2011 to decide if Southern Sudan will become an independent country or maintain the status quo within the Republic of Sudan.

Urban Standards

While the South Sudanese towns have little or no infrastructure, and that massive investment is needed to upgrade them into operational urban centers, demands an analysis relating the social-economic demand to the resources needed to satisfy that demand. The investment must be weighed against the expected benefits – the improvements expected to be achieved in terms of economic production and social wellbeing.

Under this perspective, the urban plan is significantly more complex than a simple land use map indicating where housing and building should take place. The word "integrated" is used to indicate that several factors are weighed in – population growth, economic potential, physical resources (such as land, natural features and building materials), human resources (skilled and non-skilled workers), institutional framework (legislation, regulations, procedures, etc.), logistics (transportation, communication and equipment) and, of course, financial resources.

From these analyses, estimates, and projections, the baseline options can be drawn: which are the development priorities, and to what extent investment should be made on which sector to achieve the best – and affordable – combination in the shortest period.

The available capital resources from the town's population, GOSS and external sources, must be balanced among the various sectors. The proportion of these resources that is invested is a function of the standards that are chosen by the towns.

Applying very low standards for a sector may compromise its efficiency, while opting for higher standards may result in a waste of resources. The objective is to find an adequate distribution that - within the existing resources – can optimize the economic and social benefits.

Having decided the standards to be used within the plan period it is then possible to re-organize the urban space – the physical plan – and define the corresponding level of infrastructure – the infrastructure plan.

It should be noted that the physical and infrastructure plans are insufficient, by themselves, to assure the beginning of a development process. The institutional and administrative instruments must be put in place, the workforce must be trained, the population provided with a basic health support, the economic sector must be aware of the new investment opportunities, and the government must be ready to provide the indispensable services that should characterize a state capital. These aspects will be addressed in the institutional plan.

As the urban development plan focuses on the urban environment, it gives more attention to land use, housing, land allocation and building, provision of urban services, development of infrastructure and similar aspects. For the sectors that are beyond the jurisdiction of the city and/or state government, the plan will identify the main actions that should be promoted, so that the city and state governments can negotiate their implementation with the central government and other entities. The overall implementation budget will be the focus of the capital investment plan.

Development Recommendations

There will be considerable variation in what will be proposed for each of the 10 towns – the development of a short-term, intensive and focused urban development plan seems to be the most sensible and logical approach to making the cities operate as simple yet reliable administrative and economic centers.

Individual town profiles will be tailored to benefit from their competitive advantages. According to their characteristics and potentials, the towns may develop as:

- administrative centers;
- providers of services;
- supporting nodes in the transportation system;
- rural and agro-industrial support centers;
- industrial and commercial centers;
- education centers, etc.

In principle, all state capitals will have a mix of these functions, yet in different proportions based on their capacity and development potential.

Housing and Land Use

The demand for land in the next 5-year period may double the urban area in some towns. Some of this can be absorbed within the existing urban area by infilling empty spaces and densifying - replacing large plot sizes around the city core (serviced area) by plots with smaller frontage and overall area, more suitable for a more compact development. This will reduce infrastructure costs, the provision of services and reduce average distances – the overwhelming majority of the population walks or uses bicycles for transportation.

The larger part of the demand for land will have to be met by providing plots at the town's periphery – where they will not have much more, within the short-term planning period, than having access to safe water, sanitation and electricity. It may be more adequate, for such development, to offer a mix of compact plots and larger "agro-urban" plots to stimulate small-scale agricultural production.

As a rule, the design of new housing districts should give preference to smaller, cost-efficient plots and more compact housing layouts. The archaic 1-2-3-4 design scheme should be replaced by a more pertinent land development system. There is no reason for not having a variety of plot configurations if such plots meet the accepted development standards. The cost of providing infrastructure is a function of the frontage of the plots. From the resource perspective, longer and narrower plots with small frontages are preferable to plots with the usual square format.

The design of the new housing schemes should adopt a modular, "neighborhood unit" concept, including in each module suitable areas for a primary school, green recreational space, a local market and other basic community facilities. The clustering of the residential area in such neighborhood units will make easier building and maintaining public sanitary units, providing safe water and electricity, and collecting household waste.

House and building construction should give preference to using local skills and materials. Housing design and the choice of building materials & methods (especially roofs) should be designed to alleviate high internal temperatures: properly dimensioned overhangs to shelter the walls from direct sunlight, larger openings to provide better ventilation, and roof insulation to reduce secondary radiation.

Housing development should give preference to using locally available building skills, stimulating the use of local manpower and the development of a building industry. Provision of government housing should be limited to key public-sector personnel that is required to relocate from their own home to fulfill their functions. There is no scope for a government-sponsored housing program for the general population, although access to credit and micro-credit programs should be facilitated for housing and site improvements (such as building private sanitary units).

Finally, the land market should be formalized, stimulating land development and building. No plot should be allocated without the right to land tenure. Secure property rights stimulate investment on building and home improvement.

City Center

The central area should provide space for government and other public buildings; social infrastructure; private commercial and office buildings; the central market place; parks and leisure areas; etc. A compact city center – the city core - containing these assets will concentrate the larger demand for better standards on water supply, sanitation, waste management, electricity, and communications. In principle, the city core should be a model for what the whole city will become in the future.

In general, most Sudanese towns lack distinctive urban features and the flat landscape does not present outstanding natural landmarks. To counter this situation, the design of each city core should consider introducing a more remarkable urban element that, by its individuality, can become a symbol of the city and a source of local pride.

Urban Services & PPP Approach

It is important that access to safe water and electricity should be made available to all inhabitants. Together, both services provide significant benefits to the well-being of the population, such as improved health conditions and economic growth. Affordable user charges should be collected to assure sustainability, preferably through a PPP scheme.

Other services such as waste collection and maintenance of public latrines can also be operated through PPP.

Social Services

The school and health infrastructure should be given priority in the implementation program as a pre-investment for future economic development and therefore should, therefore, be accessible to the whole urban population.

Yet investment in school buildings and clinics can become superfluous if teachers, doctors, and nurses are not available and operational conditions are not provided. All schools and health facilities should be equipped at the same infrastructure standard of the city core, preferentially with flush toilets.

Industrial Areas

According to the economic potential of each city, suitable areas in the urban periphery should be reserved for industrial use so that heavy traffic is diverted from the city center.

Traffic and Road Network

The road system should be consolidated, yet a high priority should be given to cater for pedestrian and bicycle traffic. Transportation terminals, along with ancillary maintenance, repair services, storage and warehousing facilities should be foreseen. This is an economic function that can kick off immediately and should be stimulated.

Environment

A city greening policy should be pursued with community participation, by promoting growing fruit trees and other useful plants in the open areas of the plots. Such initiative will improve the quality of food intake, and provide some additional income. It will also contribute to a more amenable living environment, and support a more comfortable micro-climate. Current restrictions on this practice, imposed by old regulations, should be removed immediately.

A tree-planting program on streets, schools and other public areas should be-implemented by the local governments, improving the urban landscape, providing shade for the pedestrian traffic and reducing excessive glare. Green open areas should also be used for community gatherings and leisure activities in the city core.

Sources:

Lucius, Douglas. "Population, Social and Economic Report". Urban Development Framework for Southern Sudan.
GibbAfrica/KwenziV3/Padco-Aecom, Nairobi, June 2006.

The Urban Component of the Energy Crisis

Co-authored with Marcos P. Pareto, M.A. Previously published on Urbanistica-PVS, La Sapienza - University of Rome, No. 51/52 (Jul-Aug. 2009).

SSRN paper # 1221622 (2008, 2013).

Preface

This paper was originally written in 2008, when oil prices had topped $100 per barrel and seemed to have no limit – prices of $200/barrel and over were foreseen. Yet a technological breakthrough in oil production (fracking), poured vast quantities of oil in the market, and the OPEC cartel increased production, making prices collapse to four times lower. Eventually, the OPEC and other oil producing countries decided to put a cap on production, stabilizing prices at a relatively low level, around $50/barrel (2016).

The question is whether these recent events made redundant this paper, pushing oil "peak" to a remote future date, or whether they merely shifted the peak oil event by a few years, not affecting the general reasoning of the paper regarding the consequences of restricted energy supply on the urban environment. To further discuss the current situation, an additional chapter was included at the end of this paper.

Introduction

The world's entire production and transportation systems – the fruits of the industrial revolution - were built upon the easy availability of fossil fuels, not only easy to extract, but of available in large quantities for an amazingly low cost. These features made fossil fuels the main and preferred means of obtaining the energy needed to fuel factories and vehicles. The low cost of energy derived from fossil fuels made the use of most other sources economically unfeasible except on special and limited conditions.

Yet somewhat obscured by the current financial and economic crisis - and perhaps in part derived from it - a fundamental change is taking place. As energy prices increase, the world's production and transportation systems can become unsustainable at the current level and the production of goods should become significantly more expensive.

In other words, the era of cheap goods available from all over the world – including food, could be finishing and another era, characterized by much more expensive goods and transportation costs may be starting. This will not only affect everybody living in the planet, but may well bring a much more stringent social crisis – including mass migrations from the poorer regions to the still affluent western world.

The progressive increase of fuel prices is not a result of a conjunctural event but a dramatic symptom of a failing supply of energy. Cheap energy was one of the main factors that allowed the explosive economic development that occurred during the last century, especially since the end of the WWII. Unfortunately, that phase seems to be over. To maintain the world development process, a new balance needs to be found between the new production and distribution profiles, considering the energy factor.

This is a normal event in the development process, yet in this case will affect almost all the productive system simultaneously and our consumption habits at an extremely fast pace. It is not the change itself – it has always been expected – but the speed of change the real issue we must cope with.

This paper intends to discuss the main factors of the energy crisis, why it is happening now and how urban development planning can contribute to alleviate the difficult transition period. Rather than being conclusive, it stresses the need for pursuing some lines of research that should be promoted on urban planning and development, adding the energy component to the conventional physical, economic and social aspects of urban planning.

The Energy Supply Issue

The world reserves of raw materials are the total amount of these materials that are physically, technically and economically available under present conditions, i.e. that can be placed in the market at the current price structure. Under these criteria, the total world reserves of fossil fuels are assumed to be around 180 billion TCE of natural gas, 300 billion TCE of mineral oil, shale and liquid gas, and 600 billion TCE of coal (all forms), adding up to the impressive amount of 1,100 billion TCE[1]. TCE means "tonne of coal equivalent", i.e. the energy produced by burning one metric ton of coal.

On the other side is the world's consumption rate, is currently around 14 billion TCE (RWE World Energy Report 2005). In other words, if consumption remains at the same level (no economic development, no population growth scenario), the

---

1   Estimates available in 2008.

present reserves would be enough to last almost until the end of this 21st century at the current price level.

Oil, gas and coal – which together provide 87% of the world's energy – are convenient, powerful and, until now, still cheap to obtain. All other forms of generating energy – from nuclear to hydro, solar, wind and others do not weight significantly on global terms.

More precisely, oil accounts for 38%, gas 23% and coal 26% of the world's energy consumption. It is foreseen that this proportion will slowly change, coal and gas increasing their share in relation to oil so that the three major fossil fuels are expected to have just about the same proportion by 2030, altogether providing 82% of the total energy production. It is also foreseen that alternative energies would gain ground, from under 1% to about 6% - a forecast as impressive as improbable.

Currently nuclear and hydro provide only 6% each, while all other sources combined provide less than 1%. Liquid fuel alternatives such as shale oil, extra-heavy oil, bio-fuels (mainly ethanol and bio-diesel), liquefied coal or gas are expected to become increasingly competitive in the near future, as conventional fuels reach higher price levels. Their supply is expected to grow from 2.5 to 9.7 million barrels per day from 2005 to 2030. Yet all these alternative sources combined are not expected to account for more than 10% of the liquid fuel demand in 2030.

The availability of fossil fuels as our main source of energy is limited by technical and economic factors. In principle, neither oil, nor gas and coal will ever be physically totally exhausted. Yet as the easier and cheaper options to find and explore are consumed, extraction costs increase dramatically, while the overall amount produced tends to be relatively smaller. For those reasons, the reserves of fossil fuels are measured in terms of their economic availability under present conditions (RWE 2005, EIA 2005).

It should be mentioned that there are also enormous quantities of "resources", a term given to fossil fuel deposits that cannot be considered reserves, because they are not feasible to explore under the current price structure or still lack adequate production technology. Such is the case of the large Brazilian very deep water "pre-salt" findings. These resources will eventually become reserves as prices go up and new exploration techniques are developed. The increased production of oil and gas from shale is a recent example. Yet one should also consider that deposits with low yield and difficult extraction consume an increasing amount of energy to be transformed into fuel, effectively reducing their net energy content (RWE 2005).

As energy prices increase, lower yield resources are upgraded to economically feasible reserves, even if no new findings are made. The critical point is when the demand equals the production capacity – the "peak". When this happens, higher prices constrain the demand, and simultaneously allow a boost in reserves, inducing an increase in supply until in due course a new peak is attained. Yet as global reserves are used, the inter-peak periods tend to shorten and, if no alternative energy sources are ready take over, a supply collapse is possible. Such scenario could bring a worldwide fuel shortage of unpredictable economic and social consequences.

Therefore, the critical issue is not when the existing reserves of fossil fuels will end – in principle they will continue to be available as prices increase – but the ultimate peak. According to some experts, oil has already started to peak (Hubbert, 1956; Deffleyes, 2002). Gas and coal reserves are bigger than oil, so the latter will tend to be progressively replaced by the former, which is foreseen for 2030. This replacement should attenuate the danger of a price explosion.

Nevertheless, this process will continue pushing energy prices higher, unless sustainable, unlimited sources, such as nuclear fusion, replace our dependency on fossil fuels as major source of energy. Yet, there is no indication that this will become reality in the foreseen future, if ever.

Higher energy prices will make alternative sources of energy economically feasible. Yet two additional issues should be considered: first, the time lag and the resources needed to tap these alternative sources and bring up production to balance the reduction in supply of fossil fuels. Secondly, the fact that industrial production and transportation costs should be higher with the increase of energy costs, bringing in a recessive trend with a consequent drop in living standards until higher efficiency and technological improvements can increase productivity and outweigh higher energy costs.

Various apocalyptic scenarios have been built under the assumption of massive shortages of essential resources such as food or energy, ranging from Malthus' timely warning[2] to the seminal "Limits to Growth" (Meadows, 1972 and 2004). While significant advances in technology and production efficiency have systematically prevented such catastrophic scenarios from happening, their warnings are sobering and should not be dismissed. In fact, if technological breakthroughs had not been discovered – and discovery is an unpredictable event – we might well be in an entirely different world.

What are the alternatives? Uranium reserves, based on production prices of up to $40/kg, are only about 40 billion TCE. Yet, contrariwise to fossil fuels, the cost of uranium ore is an insignificant part in the cost of energy produced – only about 0.1 cent/KWh, about 2-3% of the production cost. It has been estimated

2   "Essay on the Principle of Population" (1798).

that if the price of extraction and concentration reached higher levels - even to the extreme of $1,000/kg - the availability of uranium as fuel would become virtually endless, while the fuel cost would remain an almost insignificant component of the cost of nuclear energy. The use of more advanced reactors and breeder technology can further contribute to lower costs and limit fuel demand (Hopf, 2004).

The energy issue is neither the technology nor the potential availability – the critical issue are the logistic factors required to replace fossil fuels by other sustainable sources within a 40-year period. Such effort, necessary to avoid a major energy crisis, requires a serious commitment of capital, human resources, industrial organization and political will.

Estimates indicate that to supply two thirds of the foreseen 2050 demand for energy would require the construction of about two hundred nuclear power plants per year, each taking over five years of construction before becoming productive, although the adoption of standard design and equipment could probably shorten the development period and reduce costs (Murkeheide 2005).

Renewable sources, such as solar, wind power or geo-thermal should become increasingly competitive as energy costs rise and have an endless availability. Yet not only is the current production insignificant, but any massive worldwide conversion to such ecological sustainable sources seems implausible within the available time frame for replacement. Furthermore, the energy from these sources is only complementary to energy from conventional plants (uranium, hydro), requiring specific conditions to work and being more expensive to implement. Hydroelectric production is expected to increase and share, with nuclear and gas-driven plants, most of the sources for electric energy in the near future (RWE 2005).

It seems clear that high oil prices will reduce oil consumption and at the same time constrain development, which is one of the main factors pushing higher consumption. High oil prices will also stimulate the use of alternative and renewable sources. Yet it should be clear that not only cheap energy from oil will gone forever, but that the time lag until sustainable sources can become significantly productive - such as producing bio-fuels, building hydro-electric dams and installing nuclear plants - will seriously constrain energy availability for some time, regardless of the scenario considered.

Replacing two-thirds of energy production from fossil fuels to other sources by 2050 would require building about 8,000 1.5 MW power plants, at a cost of about 2.5 billion each – regardless of using nuclear, hydro, wind or any other sustainable energy source. It is assumed that by 2050 both gas and oil will be too costly to supply the energy demand and the only remaining fossil fuel available would be coal. Although using bio-fuels is possible, the demand for fertile land – required to feed 9 billion people - and the huge quantities involved should limit their use as a major source of energy.

Energy Demand Pattern

Compounding to supply constraints, the increase in demand aggravates the problem, and turns what could be a smooth transition to a more dramatic situation. Demand for energy is driven by two main factors – population growth and economic development. The world's population is estimated to grow from the current 6.9 to 9.2 billion by 2050, adding 2.3 billion people to the planet in just 40 years. Yet this increase is not evenly distributed. The industrialized nations have already stabilized their population at a little over 1.2 billion and all the expected population growth should happen in the developing nations (UN 2007). Similarly, during this same period the rate of economic development is expected to remain low (at less than 2%) in the industrialized countries, while the developing nations are expected to maintain a high 4-5% rate of economic development.

As a result, the increase in energy demand is expected to remain almost stable in the developed nations, due to its slower economic development and the use of more energy-efficient equipment. Contrariwise, consumption should increase at an exponential rate in the developing countries. Despite an increasing price pattern, the world demand for energy is expected to grow by 50% from 2005 to 2030, with the non-OECD countries accounting for about 85% of the additional demand. The total energy consumption of the non-OECD countries has already matched the consumption of the OECD countries (EIA/IEO 2007). In the cities of Asia, Latin America and Africa, new businesses are continuously being created, generating employment, and millions of people are swapping their bicycles for cars and acquiring more fridges, TVs, air conditioners, computers and all kinds of home appliances, as personal prosperity rises in line with national economic growth (ExxonMobil 2008).

The use of energy is overwhelmingly concentrated in urban areas, where 75% of the energy consumption takes place, and the urbanization trend remains firm (BP 2008). Until 2050 the world's urban population is expected to increase dramatically, from 3.5 to 6.4 billion people. But the population in the urban centers of the less developed regions is expected to increase from 2,570 million in 2010 to 5,327 in 2050. Thus, the cities of the developing nations are expected to absorb 2.7 billion new dwellers, bringing a correspondingly strong demand for housing, infrastructure, jobs and energy (UN 2007).

As such, it seems clear that while one focus of attention should be on shifting energy production from fossil fuels to sustainable sources, an equally important one is where the increase in demand will take place: the rapidly expanding urban centers of the developing nations.

Urban Development Alternatives

In the developed nations both the urban network and city sizes are almost entirely static. The regional and urban infrastructure is fully developed, limiting the possibility of a significant increase in energy efficiency. Because the possibility of physical change is negligible, improvements are limited to increasing the operational efficiency of the transportation network (both inter and intra-urban) and introducing energy conservation strategies.

Contrariwise, the cities in the developing countries of Asia, Latin America and Africa will double in size in the next forty years to cater for 2.7 billion more people. Such urban places – equaling in size to all the currently existing cities put together - present a unique opportunity to consider the energy factor when planning and building the urban spaces.

There are four main areas where urban and regional development planning can contribute to improve energy efficiency and avoid waste: the location of cities, urban size, use of space and building design.

Cities are focal points of economic activities - and this is the main single reason why urban centers develop and grow. The basic reasons for development of urban centers are to be found in the economic activities they perform in the economy and the people directly or indirectly employed by these activities. Classic urban location theory is based on the allocation of economic activities throughout the geographic space and in the distribution system (Alonso 1964, Christaller 1966, Lösch 1973, Johnson 1975), considering the cost of transportation to receive goods and raw materials (inputs) and to distribute the production to the consumers (outputs). Yet the flow of goods that justified the concept of a "central place" hierarchy of urban centers disintegrated in the twentieth century, due to the availability of extremely cheap fuels, the development of modern and efficient means of transportation and improvements on the transportation infrastructure.

Rather than based on the typology of the urban economic profile, urban centers with higher product developed faster. Economies of scale reinforced the development of primary cities and eventually of mega-cities, with populations in the range of tens of millions and attaining economic self-sufficiency regardless of their geographical location. Larger cities and metropolises mostly arise because of economies of scale, especially when the availability of human resources and necessary supporting services is essential to compete in the world market. As investments increase, more resources flow in, and the more attractive is the city for further investments, which in turn generate employment and attract more migrants.

This cycle is especially visible in the developing countries, where such resources are scarce and are frequently limited to a few regional or national centers, reinforcing the primacy paradigm. Yet the continuous expansion of city sizes does not come without a price - diseconomies of scale such as congestion, failing urban transportation, poor quality of life, pollution, higher land prices and lack of infrastructure – not to mention higher social dysfunctions such as criminality and loss of social order - can erode some of the advantages of the larger centers in favor of alternative locations (Royuela & Suriñach, 2005). Furthermore, the relative loss of importance of geographic location in urban development may need to be reconsidered as transportation costs increase, revalidating some of the original assumptions of the location theory.

Another issue of larger cities is that their higher affluence level acts as a magnet, generating strong migration flows from smaller centers and urban areas where employment if limited, income levels are lower, and opportunities are scarcer (Harris & Todaro, 1970). Indeed, the development of urban economic activities often benefits from the labor of migrants. Yet while providing mutual economic advantages, excessively fast migration flows tend to overburden urban services and to generate widespread informal settlements and squatters. Most local government policies try to alleviate such problems by improving urban conditions, such as expanding urban infrastructure and services networks and incorporating more space to cater for future urban growth. Yet such measures may eventually aggravate the problem of excessive urban size and continuous growth since the improvements made will stimulate the inflow of migrants.

Urban energy consumption profiles can vary widely. Taking four large Asian cities - Tokyo, Seoul, Beijing and Shanghai – the amount of energy consumed by industrial activities can range from 80% in Shanghai to only 11% in Tokyo, while residential consumption can vary from 37% in Seoul to only 7% in Shanghai. Beijing consumes only 8% of its energy in transportation, in contrast with 37% in Tokyo; and while Shanghai commercial activities consume only 3% of its energy, Tokyo consumes 30% - ten times as much (Doi 2005). These discrepancies make clear that other factors have a stronger influence in the energy consumption profile, such as the prevailing economic system and urban affluence, in addition to the level of development and typology of economic activities performed.

Urban transport is one of the major components in the consumption of energy. It is obvious that average distances increase as the area of the city expands - and longer distances will necessarily consume more energy. Furthermore, a road system that was designed when the city was much smaller and transportation needs more limited cannot cope with the traffic generated when it grows to a size several times larger. Enlarging main roads or building elevated highways is sometimes possible, yet at the cost of poorer urban quality. Furthermore, as the number of vehicles increases, it becomes virtually impossible to expand road sizes at surface level – not even mentioning the issue of providing parking spaces. If roads could keep increasing in size according to traffic demands, eventually all the city center would have to be demolished to make space for a giant roundabout.

To cope with increasing demand for personal transportation, especially the critical home-work-home peaks, the preferred solution has been to promote public transport and adopt mass transit solutions, like underground rail systems. Yet those systems are costly to build and operate, and do not provide more than a temporary relief from congestion. Eventually there is a point of utter collapse, which some megalopolises have already reached, having to constrain vehicle access to the more congested areas.

There is a vast demand for energy, ready to explode in the cities of the developing countries. Increasing the efficiency of land use design to reduce the demand to travel long distances and stimulating neighborhood activities and non-motorized traffic (walkways, bicycles, etc.) can result in significant energy savings. It has been demonstrated that it is possible to design "pedestrian" cities that can support more than 100,000 people without incurring on excessive densities, limiting green areas or lowering the quality of live. Such settlements do not need to eradicate personal vehicles - the car is a cherished symbol of freedom, besides providing personal comfort. The point is that by making the use of personal cars optional rather than essential, it is possible to have better cities without sacrificing quality of life or the freedom of movement.

Larger cities could be conceived combining such "urban modules", without significantly changing the concept. Cities much larger than one million could be avoided altogether - there are very few economic activities that need a labor supply that large. Yet even larger urban conglomerations can be conceived by establishing an urban network, much like the current Swiss or Dutch urban systems. Such structure of urban centers could provide a concentration of urban dwellers spread throughout a relatively small geographic space, providing the benefits of a large concentration of economic activities and resources, while taking full advantage of economies of scale without incurring in excessive congestion, pollution, long commuting periods, or high transportation costs.

Such urban development strategies could be promoted in the developing countries, providing not only significant savings in intra-urban transport, but also in inter-urban transportation, by allowing more energy efficient modes of transportation to be implemented.

Finally, the building structure can play a significant part in avoiding energy wastage by stimulating environmentally efficient design. Except the few places that have a year-round fair climate – such as Brasilia or Nairobi – most cities need heating in the winter or cooling in the summer, and very often both. Yet significant energy savings can be attained without increasing cost or sacrificing comfort by using the building materials suitable to the environment, better insulation and by designing spaces with better air flow and control of solar exposure according to the prevailing climate.

Conclusions

It seems clear that we are already facing a major crisis in the supply of energy and that the economic production model based on cheap energy needs to be revised. Whatever alternative and sustainable source of energy is preferred - and most probably all means available will need to be considered - the world economy probably will have to go through a scarce energy period, during which not only energy will be increasingly expensive, but also difficult to get. To reduce this pressure, not only alternative fuels and other energy sources need to replace current fossil fuels as main sources of energy, but attention should also focus on reducing the growth of demand, not only by applying technological improvements aiming at higher energy efficiency, but also through urban development approaches that take in consideration the scarcity of energy.

Urban areas – and particularly those that will be built in the developing countries – will account for most of the additional demand for energy in the next 40 years, absorbing 2.7 billion people and almost doubling the demand for energy. Those urban centers present a unique opportunity to apply alternative planning approaches considering location, size and land use decisions from a more expensive energy perspective. Similarly, the need to build half a billion new housing units, not including replacements, industrial and commercial buildings - a sizable investment in any count - will also present a major opportunity to implement energy-saving design concepts and building techniques, provide environmental comfort and reduce operational costs. These are unique opportunities, because the size of urban population is bound to peak in this century and thus the intensity of urban development expected in this first half of the century is not expected to ever repeat itself.

Within this context, accessibility should play a decisive role in location decisions: possibly stimulating more concentrated and economically integrated settlements, or avoiding mega cities in favor of a more comprehensive system of urban centers. Such shift in focus could change dramatically the American urban sprawl model, bringing striking repercussions in the real estate market (WSJ, 2008).

While Adam Smith's invisible hand will quickly change energy consumption habits and support a shift toward more energy efficient buildings, a massive effort still needs to be made in disseminating such design methods and building techniques, to ensure that the opportunity will not be missed by sheer ignorance. The revision of building codes is a necessary step in this direction although insufficient by itself.

On the other hand, urban development decisions in favor of expanding existing cities, building new urban centers and setting up urban infrastructure and services according to a preferred land use pattern, are continuously made by the local, regional or central authorities, who still are not aware of their role and responsibility in participating in the energy management effort.

To be sure, there is no "new" urban development approach – an urban development "recipe" considering the energy issue – which is readily available and just needs to be disseminated. A significant effort in research and development must be made, reviewing the theoretical base of urban development, combining the traditional social, cultural, economic and environmental aspects with the increasing importance of dealing with energy demand issue – a task that should be undertaken primarily by universities, research centers and practitioners in the field.

But what about shale?

Shale oil and gas became commercially feasible with the development of the fracking technique and increased dramatically the North American production. Yet does this mean that the energy crisis is dead and buried? It seems that not in the least (Dimick, 2014). Although the North American production rivals with Saudi Arabia, it's coming from reserves that are only a small fraction of the ones in the Middle East.

Output from oil fracking in the U.S. has tripled from one million barrels in 2010 to over 3 million in 2013, and the total U.S. production has risen to over 9 million barrels/day, almost the same as Saudi Arabia.

Yet fracking oil or gas from mile-deep shales is expensive. High oil prices made it lucrative investment – over one million fracked oil or gas wells exist in the U.S. With lower prices, due to the cut in production from the OPEC and other countries, fracking becomes much less competitive and drilling new wells has slowed down significantly. The issue is that shale wells have a short life – in a few years the production drops drastically. If fewer wells are drilled, the current high production capacity is sure to drop radically in short term.

What this means is that when the production drops, the prices will go up, making economically feasible drilling new wells. This is the normal economic cycle. Fuel will continue to be available, although prices will slowly tend to rise. Rather, the real issue is the size of the reserves. According to the IEA (2014), the U.S. oil supply, dominated by fracking, should begin to decline as soon as 2020. The basis for these projections are the estimates of shale oil reserves. The technically recoverable shale oil in the U.S. – the quantity that is recoverable regardless of cost - is under 60 billion barrels. That is equivalent of about only 9 years of U.S. consumption at the current rate of just under 20 million barrels/day. Yet the proven reserves – the economically feasible at current prices – are only about 10 billion barrels! In contrast, the proven reserves of the main Middle East producers – Saudi Arabia, Kuwait and the Emirates – total more than 460 billion barrels. The major supplier of oil will continue to be the Middle East, long after the U.S. fracking boom has run its course.

Price is important, as higher prices will increase shale proven reserves, but regardless of the recent U.S. production boom, the overall world scenario did not change significantly – peak oil remains in the agenda.

Sources and References

Alonso, W. Location and Land Use. Harvard University Press, 1964.

British Petroleum. "Imperial College Urban Energy Project, 2008." http://www.bp.com.

British Petroleum. "BP Statistical Review of the World Energy 2012. http://www.bp.com/statisticalreview.

Christaller, W. Central Places in Southern Germany. Prentice Hall, 1966.

Deffeyes, Kenneth. Hubbert's Peak. Princeton University Press, Princeton, NJ, 2002.

Dimick, Dennis "How long can the US oil boom last?". National Geographic, Dec 2014.

Doi, Naoko. "Urban Development and Transportation Energy Demand." Asia Pacific Research Center, 2005.

Energy Information Administration. "International Energy Outlook – 2008". http://www.eia.doe.gov/eia.

Energy Information Administration. "International Energy Annual – 2005". http://www.eia.doe.gov/eia.

ExxonMobil. "Energy Outlook", 2008. http://www.exxonmobil.com

Harris J. and M. Todaro. Migration, Unemployment & Development: A Two-Sector Analysis. American Economic Review, March 1970.

Forrester, J. World Dynamics. Wright Allen Press, 1971.

Hopf, James. "World Uranium Reserves – 2004". http://www.americanergyindependence.com.

Hubbert, M. King. "Nuclear energy and the fossil fuels." Shell publication #95. June 1956.

International Energy Agency (IEA) "World Energy Outlook 2014". London, 2014.

Johnson, E.A. The Organization of Space in Developing Countries. Harvard University Press. 1975.

Karp. J. "Cities lure some US residents from afar." Wall Street Journal, 18 June 2008, pg. 14.

Lahart, J. "Have US drivers reached filling point of no return?" Wall Street Journal, 18 June 2008, pg. 14.

Lösch, A. The Economics of Location, Yale University Press, 1973.

Meadows et al. The Limits of Growth, A Report to the Club of Rome. Universe Books, 1979; and The Limits of Growth: the 30-year update. Chelsea Green Publishing, 2004.

Muckerheide, J. "How to build 6,000 Nuclear Plants by 2050". Executive Intelligence Review, June 2005. http://www.larouchepub.com/other/2005/3225build_6000_nukes.html.

Pareto,V. and Farret, R. "Cidade e Energia – implicacoes espaciais do problema energético". Revista Projeto #37. Ed. Vicente Wissenbach. Brazil, 1976.

Royuela, V. and Suriñach. J. "Quality of life and urban size". European Regional Science Association conference papers, 2005.

RWE AG – "World Energy Report – 2005." http://www.rwe.com.

Safirova, E. et al. "Spatial development and Energy Consumption" (discussion paper). Resources for the Future, Dec 2007.

UN Population Division, "World Population Prospects: The 2007 Revision and World Urbanization Prospects".
http://esa.un.org/unpp and http://esa.un.org/unup.

Designing an Addressing System

Published as "Manual on Metric Addressing System" by the Kathmandu Metropolitan City. Kathmandu, Sept 2001.

Introduction

An addressing system is a geographic coding system. It is a method to identify and locate an urban property using a unique reference (address). Having a good addressing system facilitates the provision of urban services and the optimization of traffic and delivery routes. It also can be used to develop a land use cadaster, which in turn can enhance urban revenue. In fact, the original purpose of establishing addressing systems was to tax properties and to conscript people for the army.

The growth of cities and the convenience of making easier to locate individual houses eventually overcame the original drawbacks, addresses becoming essential not only for the government, but for the population itself to find their way. Not being able find specific destinations is not only an inconvenience, but also a continuous waste of time and effort.

Yet numerous large cities still do not have a suitable addressing system. Some do not even have a system that identifies the location of their streets and buildings.

An urban addressing system is expected be an intuitive reference system. It should be both logical and simple, so that everybody can understand it, regardless of education. It should also have sufficient flexibility to accommodate physical changes: new streets, new buildings, and all possible sub-divisions and layouts, considering that the urban environment is continuously subject to significant changes throughout time.

Traditional Addressing Systems

House numbering is a relatively modern practice. In old times, houses were identified by their name or the name of their owner, and were located with the aid of landmarks, such as a church, a market or a bridge, a geographical feature such as a river or hill, and so on. In villages, small towns and even cities, people lived in small neighborhoods and everyone was familiar with their neighbors and surroundings. There was little need for identification beyond the name of the house and a short description of where it was located. This simple method worked quite well for a long time and is still used when giving directions.

Modern house numbering was introduced in Europe in the 18th century, during the age of "reason and enlightenment". But its original purpose was not to help a stranger to find his way or for a merchant to deliver his goods. Rather, the states needed to know where people lived to force citizens to join the army and for collecting taxes to pay for increasingly expensive wars. Not surprisingly, the implementation of house numbering was unpopular - it was a clearly a means of control to oppress the population and reduce their individuality.

Yet, coincidently, the grown of urban size due to the industrial revolution, which made difficult for people to find their way beyond their neighborhoods, and the expansion of the postal system, which needed a location scheme to deliver mail, documents and parcels, made house numbering slowly being accepted (Tautner 2009). Individual addresses are now an essential part of the urban environment and street names and house numbers are only noticed when they are missing, creating a nightmare for the outsider to find his way.

Addressing systems are meant to be simple to understand, implement and maintain. Basically, there were two main approaches. The first was to define a cluster of houses – a small village, a place, a neighborhood, a block, etc. that could be easily identified, and then number all the buildings within that cluster following a sequence. If new units were built within the area, they would receive new numbers. If some buildings are demolished, their numbers would be reused in new constructions in the same place or elsewhere. Such approach is very simple and can be convenient when the place does not have many houses.

Its critical shortcoming was that when the urban fabric changed, the original numbering logic was lost. While the number can identify the unit, it does not indicate its position within the cluster. As such, when the original numbering logic is corrupted, there is no way to know where a building is except by asking around or checking one by one until the building being sought is found. When the area is intensively built-up and has numerous passageways, internal courts, multiple entrances and several floors – a characteristic of old cities - finding an individual unit in such a maze can become quite a challenging experience, usually not successful without the help of a local dweller.

The second approach, rather than using an area, refers to the road network as the first locational reference. This made more sense, since one always needs to reach the desired destination through the network of access ways: streets, roads, avenues, squares, courts, alleys, etc.

The road based addressing systems has obvious advantages over the place system. While the latter refers to an area where the units are located, the road system refers to a line, along which the buildings are located. From simple geometry, we know that two coordinates are needed to locate a point in an area, while only one is needed along a line. As such, a single number can precisely locate a unit along a road, but does not provide enough information when the unit is within a place.

Another strong argument in favor of the road based systems is that since all buildings must have an access point (entrance) from a public access way, by identifying the access road in the address, the user will know precisely from where the unit can be reached. Due to these advantages, systems based in areas or clusters tend to be progressively replaced by systems based on the road system.

These two main approaches are not the only way to locate a building – geo-based coordinate systems can identify precisely any location in the planet. Yet they need decoding and are more appropriate for computer-based geographical information systems (GIS) rather than for personal use. "Liberty Street 17, apt 2" immediately conveys the information that it refers to sub-unit 2 of the building no. 17 on Liberty Street, which is much more understandable that something like "12GT59-0-347B" which may convey the same information yet in a much more cryptic way.

While superior to the cluster or neighborhood addressing method, the conventional road-based systems are not without issues. These can be from the unprecise identification of streets or access ways, which can be difficult when the main access way to the building is not in a usual linear street, but inside a maze of alleys, courts and interlinked constructions, or when the same building faces several access ways. Likewise, quite often the house numbering scheme along a street does not follow a logical pattern, or can have its original numbering logic distorted by physical changes, like demolitions, plot sub-divisions or mergers, new buildings or the extension of the street itself.

What differs in road-based addressing systems is how the buildings are numbered along the roads. While there is consensus that the numbering should start at the beginning of the street, this is often the only thing that they have in common.

One popular yet awkward method is the horseshoe scheme, in which the numbers grow sequentially until the end of the street, then return by the other side, making the higher number be opposite to the number one. As the user does not know where the street ends and that the numbering returns by the other side, he cannot know if the nearest route to his destination is to follow the numbering until he gets to the one he wants or if he can avoid a long walk by simply crossing the road. Neither, if you reach the road in its middle by another intersecting road, if you should turn left or right - there is no logical way to find out if the numbering increases or decreases in each side except by checking carefully the direction the numbers follow on both sides of the street.

A logical improvement was the odd-even system, introduced in Philadelphia in 1790. On one side of the street all numbers are odd, and in the other side all numbers are even. The user can easily find in which side of the road he should be (odd or even) and the direction to go by checking in which direction the numbers increase or decrease. As the size of the plots can vary significantly, the numbers in each side of the road may increase at different rates and two sequential numbers can be quite distant from each other. But at least one knows the direction to go.

The odd-even numbering method is simple to use and easy to implement. At one side, conventionally on the left side of the road in the direction numbers increase, the numbering starts at 1 and follows the sequence of odd numbers: 1, 3, 5, 7 etc. until the end of the road. On the opposite side, the numbering starts at 2 and follows the sequence of even numbers: 2, 4, 6, 8 also until the end of the road. There is no interruption in these sequences - vacant sites do not receive numbers. Buildings around squares are usually numbered clockwise, sequentially.

This system is suitable while there are no major changes in the building layout or no subdivisions of sites. Indeed, it is the most commonly found around the world. Yet there are serious shortcomings - when buildings are demolished, gaps are created in the original numbering, and when new buildings are erected they need new numbers – which is impossible to provide within the existing sequence of integers. To avoid renumbering the whole street – which would be extremely inconvenient to the residents – the numbering gaps are tolerated and the numbering scheme requires the use of appendices to identify new buildings: as a, b, c; bis, ter, quater; and even using fractions such as $\frac{1}{2}$ or ¾). When buildings are combined, they often reuse the previous numbers, such as 11-17 (not including 12, 14 and 16, which are in the opposite side of the street). These adjustments distort the original concept of sequential numbering along the access way and eventually the distortions add up to a point when there is no option but to renumber the whole street, which implies on removing all the number plates and fixing new ones.

A further inconvenience is that it provides poor indication of how far the destination is. The distance from #10 to #12 can be only a few meters, but if the two adjacent buildings are built on large sites the distance between them is also be quite large. Not only that, but the relationship between the numbering of the two sides of the street is quickly lost – #1 is indeed opposite to #2, yet #101 can be very far from # 102.

The issue with most current addressing systems is not how efficient they are when established, but how they can deal with the physical changes, which continuously happen. If houses are numbered continuously, there is a problem when a new unit is built between two already numbered units – the alternative of identifying it by adding letters, fractions or "bis" can be used, but cannot be stretched indefinitely. Eventually the whole street must be renumbered.

A proper addressing system should cope with physical changes without having to renumber the buildings from time to time. Situations such as roads being extended, additional plots being created; plots being merged or subdivided; the increase or reduction of the number of buildings in the street; new building being erected on empty plots; old buildings being demolished and replaced (or not) by other constructions; et cetera. Any of these events will affect and make pointless the principle of continuous, sequential numbering.

Designing the Addressing System.

To be logic, intuitive, functional and lasting, a few basic principles should guide the design of an addressing system:

- All roads and public access ways having built properties should be clearly identified by a name or a code.
- Each building should have a unique number that identifies that unit along the public access way.
- The numbering sequence should not be affected if any building is demolished or if other buildings are erected in the same public access way.
- Individual addresses should consist of the name of the main access way (street, road, etc.) from where the unit can be reached; a unique number that identifies the unit; and, when pertinent, complementary information to clearly identify each individual unit within the same building.

Through different approaches, all existing addressing systems resolve these basic requirements except for complying with the physical change issue. This can be resolved quite easily when establishing a new addressing system. Existing systems, however, must be renumbered – but this will only be required once and can be done progressively, street by street, without having to change the numbering of the whole city at the same time.

To overcome the drawback of the conventional systems, one should not number each building unit sequentially, but by the distance (in meters or other unit) from the beginning of the public access way (street, avenue, path or equivalent) to the entrance of the unit at the access way. This is always a unique number, regardless of the number of buildings at present or in the future in the street. With the unique advantage that, even without going to the place, one knows how far is each building from the beginning of the street – a particularly useful feature when dealing with long streets.

As there are almost always two sides in all access ways, the numbering should comply with the conventional odd-even rule.

Another advantage of this method is that the numbering on each side always increases at the same rate and it is possible to figure out quite easily the distance between two buildings along the street. Building no. 210 is opposite no. 209 (or 211) and precisely 800 meters from no. 1010.

The beginning of the numbering of any street can be arbitrarily established at the point of the intersection with the street from where it starts. The number of the building is given by the distance from beginning of the street to the main entrance of the unit being numbered.

The measurement of the distance does not have to be extremely precise – if the main entrance is 131 meters from the beginning of the street and the building is on the even side it can receive indifferently number 130 or 132, without affecting the numbering rule. Two adjacent houses, with the distance between their entrances under 2 meters can simply have two sequential odd or even numbers, without affecting the system.

Empty plots should not have numbers because it is not known where the entrance of the building(s) will be. A plot can be easily positioned by referring to the building immediately before or after it. If a building is demolished, its number simply disappears. Otherwise, if new buildings are erected, the position of the entrance of each unit will define the number it will receive.

Since the entrance to the building is the reference point to his number, there is no logic inconsistence in allocating new numbers to new buildings and eliminating old numbers from demolished buildings – whatever happens to any site or building has no consequence on the numbering of any other building in the same street.

Furthermore, it avoids almost entirely the need to create awkward suffixes to identify new buildings or any such complications. The system is simple, logic and intuitive. It can be easily understood by children and by strangers to the neighborhood. It fulfils all the requirements of a modern addressing system and avoids the shortcomings of most other systems. In short:

- It is an easy to use addressing system for residents and visitors;
- It is easy and cheap to implement.
- It is built on a consistent logic framework, avoiding the need for periodic renumbering and providing remarkable stability. It can be easily linked to systems that rely on a stable property identification and location system, such as the land use cadaster and the tax collection system.
- It facilitates the operation of the postal service and of other personal and commercial delivery systems, the operation of public utilities, and improves the efficiency of emergency services such as ambulances and security vehicles.

The Implementation Process

Identifying the access ways

Before numbering houses and buildings, the process begins with setting up a clearly identifiable road system, by assigning to each public access way an exclusive identifying name, number or code.

The street naming process starts from an arbitrary point, which is defined as the origin. Usually, since the city expands from the center outward, the origin is placed at the center of the city, but any landmark may be chosen as the origin.

The length of each street is established by common sense. If after an intersection, the street keeps the same direction and characteristics, the street is the same and should keep the same name. If not, it should take a different name.

If after an intersection, it splits in two or more branches, only the one in that follows closely the same direction and characteristics of the street can be considered its continuation. All the other branches should be named as different streets.

Defining the starting point

After all access ways are identified, one must define which end should be the starting point, from where the numbering will begin.

The usual rule is to place the beginning at the extremity that is closer to the origin, since most cities then to grow from the center outward. Thus, all the radial roads have their numbering starting from the center of the city (or the established origin). Secondary streets start at the intersection with the main road. If one is lost, the way to the center of the city can always be found by following decreasing numbers, from one street to the other.

A secondary landmark, such as a river, or a geographical orientation should also be chosen, to resolve eventual doubts in setting up where the beginning of each street should be (in doubt, numbering increases toward inland from the shore, or toward a cardinal point, or other reference point, as preferred).

The public access ways that are not streets, such as squares or circles, should have their own names. Following the basic rule, the numbering should always start from the intersection closer to the origin.

Assigning numbers to buildings

A few rules are needed to avoid confusion:

- The conventional odd/even numbering on each side of the road should be maintained - from the beginning of the road, the right side of the street should have even numbers and the left side the odd numbers.

- A unique number should be allocated to all buildings that are currently used for living and other purposes. The number of each building will be determined by the distance (in meters or other suitable unit) from the beginning of the road to the entrance of the building/plot, respecting the odd and even rule. If the distance is 79 meters and the building is in the even side, it will be either 78 or 80. Likewise, if the distance is 80 meters and the building is on the left side, it can be either take the no. 79 or no. 81.

- A single entrance should be identified for each building and thus gets only one number. If a building has two or more independent entrances or entrances from different access ways, one of them must be selected as the main entrance and the numbering will be allocated based on the position of that entrance. If there are several independent buildings in the same plot, each with its own independent entrance from the street, each building should have its own number.

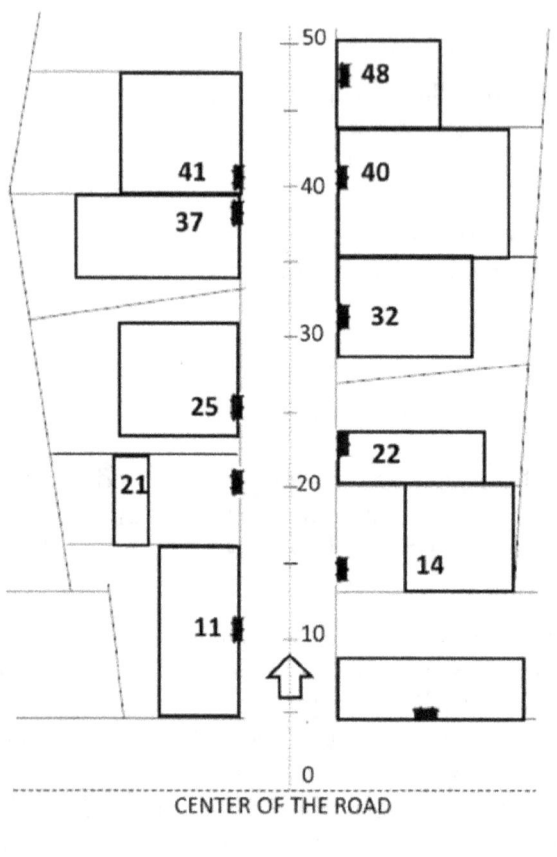

Figure 11 - Linear numbering

- Empty plots are not assigned numbers until a building permit is awarded.
- Demolished buildings lose their number.

While numbering buildings in a linear road is very straightforward, in numerous cases, especially in old cities, buildings and roads are found with all possible geometric formats and some additional clarification may be needed.

Road junctions:

At a junction, both streets should maintain their own numbering scheme, each one numbering only the buildings that have entrances to it, thus disregarding the buildings that have entrance to the other street.

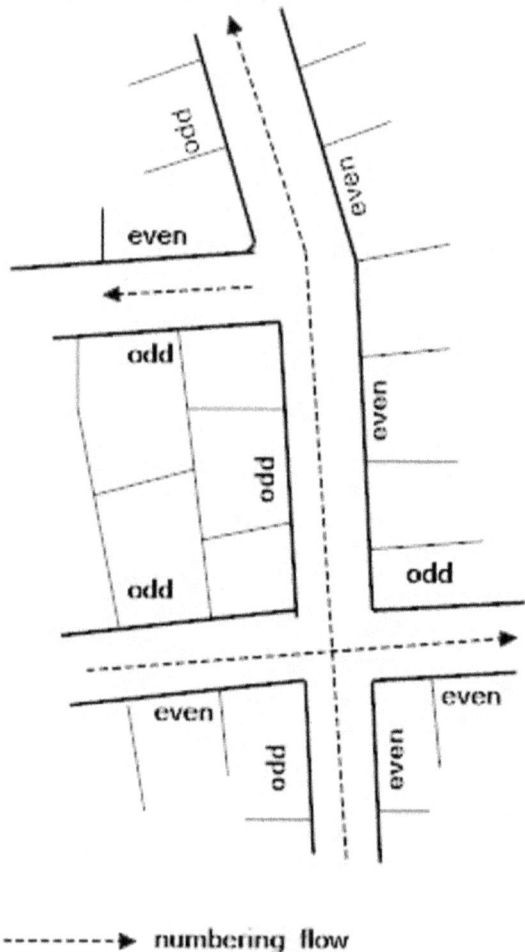

Figure 12 - Numbering flow at junctions.

Bulges and dead ends:

A "bulge" is when the street widens on one or both sides, making the frontage larger than the measuring line at the middle of the street and thus losing correspondence to it. The same happens when the street has a small alley without exit – the correspondence with the measuring line is lost.

In this case, a secondary numbering is needed. This, arbitrarily, is the center of an imaginary line lining up the two edges (points A and B in the map) of the bulge, as it was a single property following the frontage of the other buildings in the street. The position of the center of this line (point C) in relation to the measuring line of the street will provide the main number to the all the buildings in the bulge. All the properties inside the bulge will have that same number (in the example, no. 37), plus a corresponding number to identify each one. This additional number, to keep the system consistent, is the distance of the entrance of each property to the beginning of the bulge (point A), following the odd/even principle.

Thus, these properties will be numbered 37/5, 37/15, 37/21 and 37/33 in the example (Fig 13). After the bulge finishes (point B), the street numbering continues normally. If eventually the street is aligned and the bulge disappears, the numbering of the street will not be affected except for the properties within the bulge.

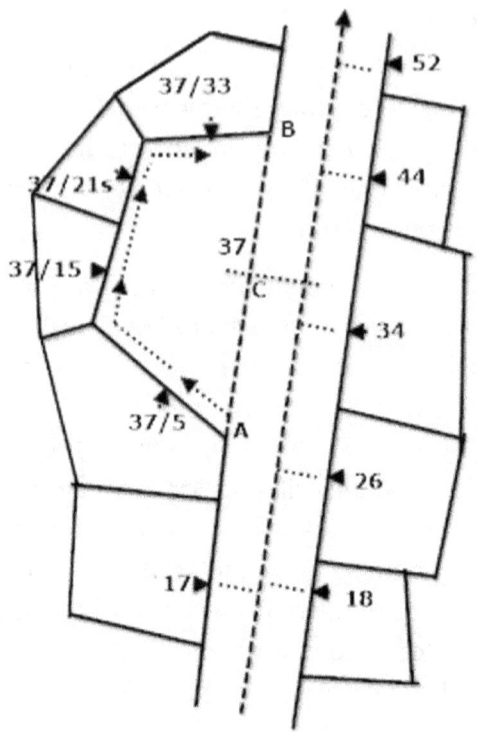

Figure 13 - Numbering a bulge

This procedure can be used to number buildings that do not follow the street frontage line. It can also be applied to small dead ends or culs-de-sac that do not have their own name.

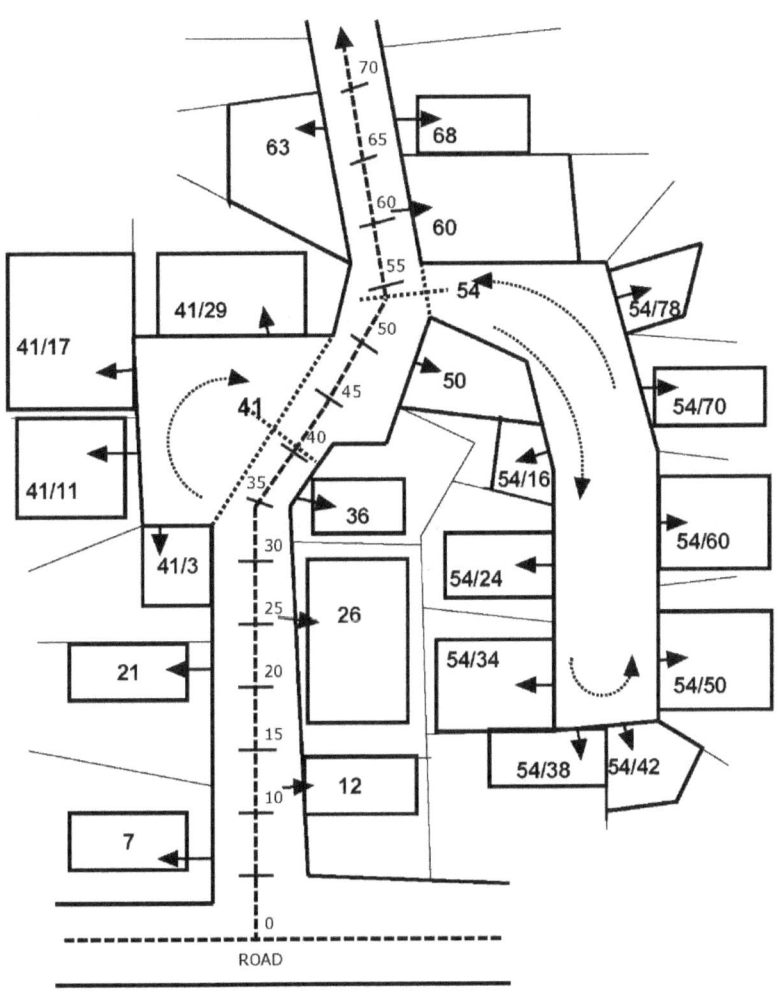

Figure 14 - Numbering flow on a bulge and a cul-de-sac.

Closed courts

A closed court is a variation of the bulge/cul-de- sac and the same numbering scheme should be used.

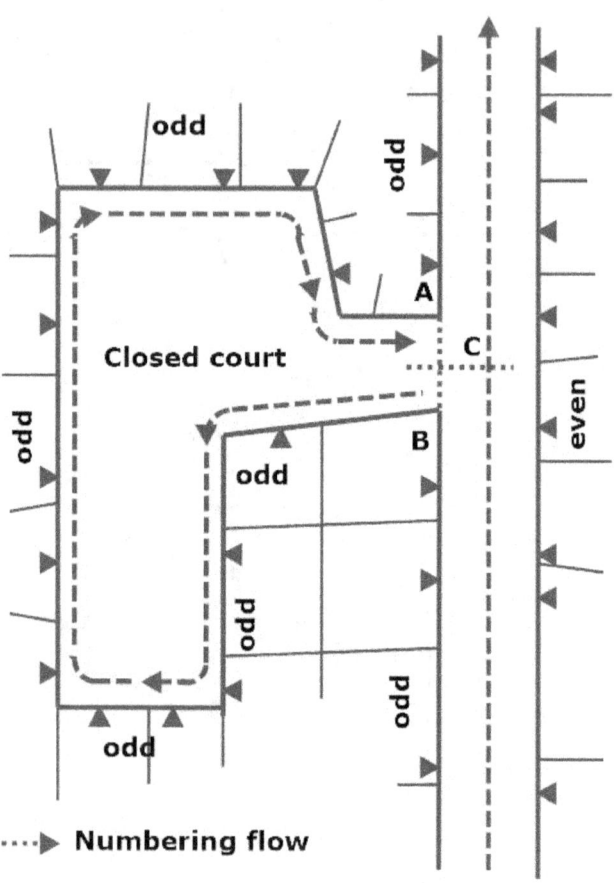

Figure 15 - Numbering flow in a closed court

Squares and circles

When there is a small square in a side of the street, it can be numbered as a bulge. If it large, it should have its own name. The numbering should start at the beginning of the square (entrance point closest to the origin) and the numbering should follow the odd/even rule on each side. The same numbering system can be applied even if the square/circle has intersections with other streets. When the square is closed, i.e. has access to only one street, the odd/even numbering stops at a point roughly opposite to the entrance point. Otherwise, the numbering should flow on each side up until reaching the opposite access.

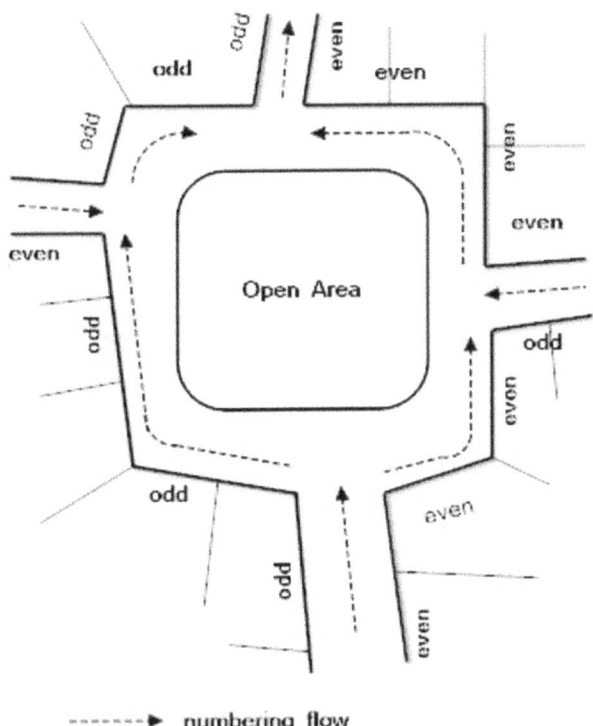

Figure 16- Numbering flow in a square

97

Building clusters and subdivided buildings

A cluster of buildings located within a compound with a single entrance shall have a single number allocated for the compound, according to the general building numbering rule. Each unit inside the compound may have a secondary number.

If a building is subdivided into more than one unit (such as apartments or shops), each independent unit should have a secondary identification number.

When there are several floors, the number of each unit should have three digits, the first one indicating the level (floor). In each floor, the numbering of the units should start from the lift or staircase (access point to the level) and be numbered clockwise using the two remaining digits to identify the unit. As such, the unit number 403, would indicate the third unit to the right from the staircase, at the fourth floor. Ground level units are numbered as being the first floor (1xx).

Sources and References

Tantner, Anton, 2009. "Addressing the Houses – The introduction of House Numbering in Europe". Histoire et Mesure, Ed. EHESS, Paris. 2009. Vol XXIV-2 pp 7-30.

American Society of Planning Officials "Street Naming and house numbering systems", Chicago April 1950. Report No. 13.

Farvacque-Vitkovic, Godin, Leroux, Verdet & Chavez. "Street Addressing and the Management of Cities" The World Bank, Washington, 2005.

About the Author

Vittorio Emmanuel Pareto was born in Rio de Janeiro in 1937, from a Genoese patrician family. He graduated in architecture from the University of Brazil (1962) and post-graduated in tropical architecture at the Architecture Association, London (AA Trop. Dip, 1965). Returning to Brazil, he joined the Federal Housing and Urban Development Agency (SERFHAU, 1965-1974) reaching the positions of general secretary and adjunct superintendent. During his tenure, the agency generated over 300 urban plans, including nine metropolitan centers[1], and established the first urban planning courses in Brazil. He led the Secretariat of Local Development, as adjunct general secretary of the Ministry of Interior (1974-1975) and was the head of the Housing and the Infrastructure Research Department of the National Research Council (1975-1982), both in Brasilia, monitoring urban development and promoting research on housing and urban development in the Brazilian universities and research centers.

Early in 1983, he was awarded a PhD from the University College, London (DPU/UCL) on urban and regional planning, pursuing his research activities as a post-doctorate scholar at the University of California's Environment Center in Berkeley (1983). Soon after, he was recruited by the UN Center for Urban Settlements (Habitat) in Nairobi, Kenya (1983), to join a team developing a set of microcomputer applications for planning.

His first consulting assignments, through Habitat, were to provide support to INGALA (Ecuador) in preparing a sustainable environment tourism plan for the Galapagos archipelago (Ecuador, 1985), and to develop a monitoring and cost control system for the

---

1   All metropolitan regions, except Rio de Janeiro.

Brazilian Popular Housing Companies (Brazil, 1986). Following, he was chosen team leader for the Karachi 2000 Master Plan project (Pakistan, 1988-1989), when several planning models were developed for planning analysis and monitoring. Returning to the USA, he joined the Center of Applied Social Studies of the University of Boston as a post-doctorate scholar, and taught microcomputer-based planning techniques at the Master of City Planning course, of the Metropolitan College (USA, 1989-1992). He left Boston to head a World Bank project in Lahore, Pakistan, preparing master and infrastructure plans for ten cities in Punjab (Pakistan, 1993-1994).

Having established his career as an international planning consultant, he decided to shift residence from Brazil to Italy, settling down with his family in Aosta, a picturesque city in the Italian Alps, near the Mont Blanc tunnel.

He continued to participate in international projects, as planning expert in a flood control project for Eastern Bangkok (Thailand, 1995); designing a primary school infrastructure plan in Cambodia (1996); providing technical assistance to the government of Cape Verde in upgrading the conditions of the main cities of the archipelago (1996); and as team leader of the Hue Urban Development Plan (Vietnam 1997).

He returned to Africa as team leader of the Greater Maputo Structural Plan project (Mozambique, 1998-1999), and from there went to Asia, as team leader of the Kathmandu Valley Mapping Program (Nepal 1999-2003), a large European Commission project to improve the conditions of Valley, where he designed and implemented a new addressing system, among other activities.

He was called back to Africa by the World Bank as institutional strengthening expert, to assist to the Building Department of Kampala City (Uganda, 2004), and returned to Kampala in the following year, now as team leader of a large environmental project, where he designed a sustainable program to improve the squatter conditions (Uganda, 2005). Still in Africa, he was team leader of the South Sudan Infrastructure Project, where he prepared a program to provide basic infrastructure and operational capacity for the ten future provincial capitals (South Sudan, 2006). For his continuous activities in Africa he was granted the Grand Cross of the Order of the Crown, awarded by king Kigeli V (Rwanda, 2009).

Vittorio was further engaged by the World Bank in preparing a coastal zone environmental project (Albania, 2006-2007), and in capacitating the local authorities of Damascus, Aleppo, Latakia and Deir-Ezzor, on replacing the central government in performing urban planning tasks (Syria, 2006-2008).

Retiring from active professional life, Vittorio now dedicates his time to genealogy studies, writing, cooking and painting. He published a book on the genealogy of his wife's Norwegian and Danish ancestors (The Flagstad, 2011), and two cookery books (The Cookbook, 2012 and The Brazilian Recipe Book, 2017). He is currently publishing his research on the origin of his family, which can be traced back to the end of Carolingian Empire (late 800's) and was the main theme of two historical romances - Anne of Ardennes and The Count of Montferrat (2017) - authored by his elder son (also called Vittorio Pareto).

Vittorio is a knight of the Equestrian Order of the Saint Sepulcher of Jerusalem, of the Order of Saints Maurice and Lazarus of the House of Savoy, and was awarded the Grand Cross of the Order of the Wing by H.H. Duke D. Duarte of Braganza. He has been married since 1959, having three sons, two of which live in Massachusetts (USA) and one in Mexico.